Discovering
LONDON'S GUILDS AND LIVERIES

John Kennedy Melling

Citizen and Poulter

Shire Publications Ltd.

ACKNOWLEDGEMENTS

Thanks are due to the Guildhall Library; the Corporation of
London Public Relations Department; the City Livery Club;
Miss Nicolette McKenzie; Donald A. Rumbelow, Editor of
City; Ede and Ravenscroft Ltd.; Whitbread & Co. Ltd. (cover
and plate 1); Ian Cook, for taking the photographs (plates
2-13, 19); and to many of the clerks of the livery companies.
The coats of arms of the London Companies (plates 14-18) are
reproduced by courtesy of the City Livery Club and do not
show certain recent alterations made in a few cases.

This historical survey is not a guide-book, is not sponsored
or supported by any City organisation, and the approval or
opinion of no authority, individual or Guild has been sought or
desired in whole or in part. Questionnaires were sent to all the
Companies. Some were very helpful, providing books or bro-
chures with the answers, suggesting interviews, tours of inspec-
tion, and, in one case, an invitation to a Court Dinner. A few
Companies were less co-operative and some did not reply at all.
The sections on pages 19 to 86 are mixtures of the answers and
the author's own researches. No Companies have been asked to
approve their section. Half a dozen asked to see their section.

CONTENTS

HISTORICAL INTRODUCTION

' An Haberdasshere and a Carpenter,
A Webbe a Dyere and a Tapicer—
And they were clothed alle in o liveree
Of a solempne and a great fraternitee.
Wel semed ech of hem a fair burgeys
To sittem in a yeldehalle on a deis.
Everich, for the wisdom that he kan,
Was shaply for to been an alderman.'

When Geoffrey Chaucer (c. 1340-1400), son and grandson of
Vintners, started writing *The Canterbury Tales* around 1386,
it was most appropriate that these perhaps slightly mocking
and ambiguous words appeared in the prologue of an epic
poem describing a journey from a capital city of guilds and
liveries, as he may have been listing them, to another city
with a livery tradition equally strong in a summarised form,
as Chaucer might have meant.

Obviously the tradition of one thousand years, common to
the Eastern and Western worlds, and the subject of two
dozen bulky tomes and innumerable individual histories,
cannot be completely covered in this handbook. This is an
aperitif to more solid and lengthy fare, or a brief refreshment,
self contained, for those desiring more than a general introduction. It is some years since there has been a paper-backed
or pocket-sized book on London's guilds. Visitors to the City
of London, British and foreign; after-dinner speakers; students;
those considering taking up the livery; present liverymen,
desirous of learning something of the roles and traditions;
those who feel that a knowledge of the subject is a pre-
requisite for countering ill-informed criticism: to all of these,
this book sets out to attract and interest, and in so doing to
impart some of the pride felt by liverymen in the world's
greatest livery traditions in the world's greatest city.

By its very nature the livery system is universal. The wearing
of a livery or uniform, by retainers, was an obvious form of
identification, for both barons and bishops, and in churches
and universities livery is both useful and compulsory. The
term ' livery ' embraced food as well as clothing. Guilds may
take different forms; there are merchant guilds whose members'
mercantile interests may be in direct opposition to those of the
craft guilds. There are the aristocratic guilds and the middle-
class guilds. There are those guilds which are strong enough
to stand alone, compared with those which link themselves

for strength into a fraternity. Finally, guilds may be formed for reasons of religion, fellowship, or common interests in trade. To appreciate better London's leading role in livery we must first examine other cities and other lands.

Chaucer may have been slightly mocking in lumping together all those livery guilds in the one livery or uniform, or he may have been implying they were joined together in a fraternity of common aims, perhaps religious, like the Ludlow palmers. We shall see that all the livery companies of London have maintained separate existences throughout, although they stemmed from a particular church. Let us start therefore with Canterbury, the city to which Chaucer's liverymen were on pilgrimage.

A city like Canterbury had about forty-five trades and crafts, none of them strong enough numerically to form individual guilds; the oldest of these is held to be the Smiths and Armourers. The actual deeds of incorporation of some fraternities are in the city archives, including the Apothecaries, Grocers, Chandlers, and Fishmongers, dated 1568-69, and the Physicians, Surgeons and Barbers, dated 1497-98 and 1543-44, and very significantly and appropriately their wardens were always presented to the mayor and town clerk 'To give them their oath after the custom of London'. London government and London livery together were the fountain not only of the British livery movement but of world democratic government.

The city of Preston has a tradition unique in Britain. 'Once every Preston guild' is the northern equivalent of 'Once in a blue moon', because from 1328 the Preston guild has taken place every twenty years with the solitary exception of a ten-year break at the time of the Second World War; Preston's first charter was granted in 1100, when the Wool Combers and Weavers were incorporated. Every twenty years the burgesses renew their freedom at a colourful traditional ceremony, when the freedom must also be taken up by all men born since the last Preston guild. In September 1972 I watched four generations in one family, or perhaps a young father with two or three sons born since 1952, all renewing or taking up their freedom. The original guilds in Preston included the Stone Masons, Free Masons, Engineers, Corn Millers, Shoe Makers or Cordwainers, Spinners and Weavers, Saddlers, Soap Makers, Goldthread Workers' Guild, Coach Builders and Gardeners.

Bristol is one of the cities with the livery tradition as well as the Societies of Merchant Venturers, which received a charter from Edward VI in 1552 and were to be responsible for most of the exploration and exploitation of North America —for example the charter granted in 1609 to the London and Bristol merchants for the plantation of Newfoundland. York and Norwich are two other cities with livery traditions, whilst the transfer of the Cutlers' trade to Sheffield resulted in the unique position of the Master Cutler of Hallamshire.

Scotland has a strong tradition of craft guilds. The Company of Merchants of the City of Edinburgh dates from 1505 when James IV became a member of the Guild of Merchants and in 1681 the company received its royal charter from Charles II; the company administers charities and is represented at many differing functions, its members being burgesses and guild brethren of the city, entitled to take part in the election of the Lord Dean of Guild. Glasgow had fifteen Incorporations with a seven-hundred-year history, a Letter of Guildry signed 1605, the Trades House completed in 1794 and the fraternity tradition. The guilds were: Hammermen, Tailors, Cordiners, Maltmen, Weavers, Bakers, Skinners, Wrights, Coopers, Fleshers, Masons, Gardeners, Barbers, Bonnet Makers and Dyers and the early casualty of the Mariners and Fishers. The Hammermen include Blacksmiths, Cutlers, Goldsmiths, Saddlers, etc. and although the membership now consists entirely of professional and businessmen, it is customary for them to join the most appropriate guild. Stirling was one of the four burghs to have a merchant guild, later locked in combat with the craftsman guild.

Abroad there have been guilds from the time of the Crafts' Guild of Silversmiths mentioned in the Acts of the Apostles, chapter 19, verse 25. In Germany during the twelfth and thirteenth centuries the aristocrats formed the *Minnesingers* and in the fourteenth and sixteenth centuries the middle classes formed the *Meistersingers* immortalised in Wagner's opera, and significantly we find that the *Feste-du-Pui*, a singing contest, was to spread from France to Flanders and England around 1300; when the German guilds disappeared it was not until 1848 that the *Innungen* were to make a much lesser impact. France has had *Les Campagnons du France* for five hundred years with initiations, offices, and craft-governing rules. Zurich had thirteen guilds in the year 1336 (dissolved 1798, reformed 1803) but from 1866 they have been of a purely social nature, particularly at the Spring Festival, the *Sechselauten* or 'Six O'Clock Chimes'. The medieval guilds were named Saffron, Tomtit, Smithy, Loaf, Tanners, Shoemakers, Ram, Carpenters, Tailors, Boatsmen,

Camel and Balance and the modern titles show that each is a fraternity, under the titles *Saffran, Schneidern, Meise, Weggen, Waag, Schmiden, Gerbe-und-Schuhmacher, Widden, Zimmerleuten, Schiffleuten, Kambel, Constaffel*. Belgium has its guild of *Brasseurs*. Luxembourg, like France, had its original guilds abolished in the early 1790s at the start of the French Revolution. China has had guilds from the time of Marco Polo and even today has its Beggars' guild with a 'king of beggars'! In the eleventh century the Vikings' Merchants' Guilds foreshadowed the Hansa Organisation.

Turning back to London, there is little link between the Saxon guilds under various names and the guilds as we now know them. We have seen that the formation of a guild is based on religious, trade, or fraternal lines, and if we consider a fraternity like Corpus Christi in All Hallows, Bread Street, and realise that most of the salters lived and operated in that area we can see how all three reasons can apply simultaneously. London still has a remarkable number of churches and the medieval city, as in Europe, naturally had each different craft in one area. Thus, in London, Poultry is the street where Poulters were found.

Whatever the basic reason for the formation of a guild merchant, and various authorities hold different theories, the membership of each fraternity would tend to be confined to that one particular craft. To this day the official title of the Merchant Taylors' Company is the Guild of Merchant Tailors of the Fraternity of Saint John Baptist in the City of London. An organisation of this type would be a help and comfort to its members in many ways as it developed. Masses or prayers would be said for deceased members; a funeral of a member would be attended, on penalty of a fine, by every member of his guild, and the coffin would be covered by an impressive pall; members guilty of bad workmanship might find themselves fined or even cast out of the guild (the expression 'sent to Coventry' is held to be derived from members rejected by their company, being unable to trade in London and having to journey to the nearest town or borough where free craftsmen could operate); where the company had a hall, members would gather for regular business meetings or to attend services in their private chapel (authorities are not agreed on the number of guilds having private chapels, but only one, the Mercers, still has one); the system of indentures or binding of apprentices would assist members in their businesses and ensure adequate training; and finally the members could progress through the various stages in the guild and take part in the democratic procedures in the city elections. Some of these functions we shall now look at in more detail because they still form a major part of the life of the livery company.

The lowest rank is that of Freeman. Formerly it was not possible to become a freeman of the city of London without first acquiring the freedom of a livery company. The procedure is now for the freedom of the chosen company to be applied for by servitude, by patrimony or by redemption (i.e. purchase). After the oath of loyalty one receives the certificate of the freedom of the company. One takes this to the Chamberlain of the Corporation of London and after the oath of loyalty there, the Roll is signed, the right hand of friendship extended, and the certificate of freedom received in a red case. This is taken back to the livery company to apply for the livery itself—but with some companies there is the intermediate stage of Yeoman. In due course by seniority one is eligible for the Court of Assistants and thereafter one can go through the various degrees of wardens to Master.

It is normal for livery gowns to be worn by the masters and wardens on official occasions. When the freeman applies for the livery, the gown is put on his shoulders at the meeting of the court where he is admitted. Formerly livery gowns, which used to be of bright tones, were worn at Common Council meetings of the City of London but this was changed in 1761 to a mazarine (blue) silk gown with fur-trimmed sleeves, worn only at the first Court of a new mayoralty and on ceremonial occasions.

The apprenticeship system is perhaps one of the finest ways of training a young man, and even today the Institute of Chartered Accountants rightly insists that five-year articles are the only way to become a chartered accountant after passing the requisite examinations. The conduct of apprentices was governed by the livery company but so was the liveryman who had taken the apprentice, whom he was obliged to supply with meat, drink, apparel and other necessaries of life.

The control of standards of work of members of a livery company has been compared, perhaps not very accurately, with the work of a modern consumer council. Where livery companies were entitled to conduct searches, work of an inferior standard could be publicly burnt and the offending trader sometimes received further ignominy: for example, a Baker might find himself dragged through the streets of London on a hurdle with the inferior loaf around his neck! Strangely enough it was the fear of being charged with low weight that caused bakers to put thirteen loaves in the dozen, thus giving rise to the present-day phrase 'baker's dozen'. We shall see in the individual chapters that some companies, notably the Goldsmiths and Fishmongers, still do apply these rigorous quality controls.

The greatest privileges of liverymen are the Common Hall. Every Midsummer Day and Michaelmas Day, on precept from the clerk of his company to attend Common Hall at the Guildhall, he arrives, to see a barrier of gates stretched across the courtyard, each marked with five or six of the eighty or so livery companies. His own beadle will be behind the gate to make certain that non-liverymen shall not pass. The privilege of liverymen to attend Common Hall, provided that the electors are freemen and liverymen of at least one year's standing, was confirmed in 1725. Once inside he finds a seat in the hall in the all-male audience, wives by courtesy being allowed to sit at the back, but taking no part in the proceedings. (Women are entitled to apply for the freedom of a company or the freedom of the City of London; Queen Elizabeth II is a freeman of the City and a few interested women are on the council. Women at one time appeared frequently on livery companies' rolls of members and even today there are a few in certain companies.) After the procession of the masters of the companies, the aldermen, in traditional livery and attended by beadles, the officers of the Corporation, the Lord Mayor and the sheriffs, the appropriate elections take place.

Midsummer Day sees the election of the two sheriffs (the aldermanic candidate, a serving alderman, and the lay sheriff who may, however, be a member of the Common Council), City Chamberlain (the rules for which were altered in 1973), the bridge masters and the ale conners. On Michaelmas Day the election is for the Lord Mayor only.

Some of the voting rights of the liverymen have been whittled away by the vagaries of central government. 1918 saw the abolition of the liveryman's right to exercise his parliamentary franchise, but grudgingly allowed those with a business premises qualification to be on a separate list of liverymen in the register and to vote as such; the special register contained 740 names in 1947. 1948 saw the abolition of the business premises qualification.

In the fifteenth century, Common Hall, or the congregation, was attended by Common Council men and leading citizens, reinforced in 1467 by masters and wardens of companies. Eight years later the liverymen replaced the men from the wards. Common Hall is the largest gathering of citizens for municipal purposes; although only liverymen may attend, and although the Court of Aldermen must grant a livery to a guild, it was held in 1775 that the guilds are not part of the Corporation, which some of them antedate: the Lord Chief Justice said: ' . . . Fraternities, companies, and guilds which make a part of the City, though not a part of the Corporation of the City originally . . .'

The Corporation is a separate authority to the Greater London Council and City of Westminster: it administers 677 acres, the 'Square Mile', four Thames bridges, many parks outside London and a superbly efficient police force, with such great financial acumen that City ratepayers do not feel the expense of items which elsewhere they have to pay for.

The livery companies have collectively influenced the tide of history. Much is owed to the enterprise, and cash, of the Merchant Venturers. There have been other colonisations, after the livery companies had been the recipients, or perhaps victims, of an elaborately worded prospectus. It was their enterprise and cash that colonised Ulster, gave it many amenities and controlled its destinies until the end of the nineteenth century. Again it was livery enterprise that did much to colonise the state of Virginia, and in more recent times, some companies helped with the financing of the abortive groundnut scheme and the agricultural colonisation of Rhodesia.

On many occasions livery cash supplied ships, sailors, soldiers and arms for royal emergencies, frequently selling their plate to raise the cash. Further emergencies came from the more ruthless and greedy monarchs, particularly Elizabeth I and the Stuarts, the latter devising the scheme of calling in the charters and making the companies buy them back again.

The livery companies have always been staunch supporters of charity, many of them maintaining almshouses in different parts of the country and giving financial help to liverymen and freemen experiencing hard times, or to the widows and children of deceased members. Without this help, it is obvious that a heavy additional burden would fall on the State.

On the educational side the livery companies' contribution to British welfare is incalculable and beyond all value. Under the individual chapters will be found some of the many huge gifts and foundations, ranging from the gift of the Goldsmiths' Company of Goldsmiths' College to London University—a considerable saving to the taxpayer, to some excellent public schools, controlled for centuries by individual companies and which have given the nation many great men, and countless donations to schools and colleges. The City and Guilds Institute (more properly Guilds and City!) owes much to the livery companies' tens of thousands of pounds to allow its formation, establishment, and efficient running.

There have been critics of the system, most apparently stemming from lack of knowledge or envy. Any institution, be it Church, university, government, BBC, business, City of London, the livery companies themselves, comes under attack, and in the 1880s there were some remarkable books suggesting the abolition of the livery companies. Through the promptings of various liberal demagogues, including a writer and MP called Joseph Firth Bottomley Firth, a royal commission was set up under the Earl of Derby, with Firth as a member. The evidence brought before the commission was voluminous, detailed, courteous and impressive and, if read thoroughly, proves a complete justification of the livery companies' operations. Many of the companies presented comprehensive evidence, and among those who spoke for them were the President of the Royal Society, Lord Chancellor Selbourne (a third-generation Mercer) and Sir Frederick Bramwell FRS. Some idea of the negotiations of this commission can be gleaned by reading the press reports issued in its name by its clerk, without prior approval of Lord Derby, and afterwards repudiated.

Finally, from the thirteenth century onwards, it could be argued that the ambition of every freeman and liveryman is to serve as Lord Mayor of the City, provided his funds run to it. This office, from the year 1192, has been unique in British and European history, for the rights, powers, traditions and duties attached. Outside the City, the Lord Mayor ranks as an earl and as a national figure, and in the City he takes precedence over everyone except the reigning sovereign. The Lord Mayor, the Mansion House, and the Court of Aldermen are outside the province of this book, but it should be remembered that the Lord Mayor has submitted himself to the electors on three occasions: first as a candidate for the voters of his ward for the office of alderman, unlike other authorities where the aldermen are elected by the councillors; secondly he will have been elected by the liverymen in Common Hall as a sheriff: thirdly the liverymen in Common Hall will have nominated him for Lord Mayor, prior to the final selection by the Court of Aldermen. It will be noticed that another proof of democracy in the City of London is not only the election of aldermen but the election of sheriffs who elsewhere are 'pricked' by the Sovereign.

The Lord Mayor's procession every November is one of the outstanding traditional pageants, with the golden coach drawn by Whitbread's superb Shire horses and the colourful floats. In the past the livery companies contributed elaborate floats, normally in praise of the Lord Mayor or the King, and so solidly built that they have served for several years, bearing beautiful damsels, attendants and dancing men, and drawn by splendid horses, whilst gifts of fruit or tobacco were thrown to the crowds. In 1703 Ned Ward, the London Spy, described somewhat cynically the procession for Lord Mayor Sir John Parsons, a Brewer and MP for Reigate: ' . . . a fellow riding a cock horse upon a lion, but without either boots or spurs . . . At the base of the pedestal were seated four figures representing (according to my most rational conjecture) the four principal vices of the City, viz. Fraud, Usury, Seeming-Sanctity, and Hypocrisy'.

Thomas Hood (1798-1845) was to write several poems on this subject, with greater affection, and the opening stanzas of one of them read:

> ' How well I remember the ninth of November,
> The sky very foggy, the sun looking groggy,
> In fact, altogether pea-soup colour'd weather,
> Shop-windows all shutter'd, the pavement all butter'd,
> Policemen paraded, the streets barricaded,
> And a peal from the steeple of Bow!
> Low women in pattens, high ladies in satins,
> And Cousins Suburbans, in flame-colour'd turbans,
> Quite up to the attics, inviting rheumatics,
> A great mob collecting, without much selecting,
> And some, it's a pity, are free of the City,
> As your pockets may happen to know! . . .
> Such hustle and bustle, and mobbing and robbing,
> All, all to see the Lord May'r's show!'

In 1401 we find traces of minstrels in the Lord Mayor's Show; in 1800 Nelson joined the procession from Westminster to Guildhall before attending the banquet and receiving a sword of honour. Cleopatra's Needle once formed a highlight; it had just arrived in England after an eventful voyage, during which the ship towing it had lost the Needle in its cylinder crossing the Bay of Biscay!

Traditionally the Thames was used for the procession until 1856, when the City ceased to be conservators of the Thames. The Lord Mayor's visits to the Crow Stone on the foreshore at Westcliff also stopped. In the days of the Restoration the *Folly,* a large hulk moored off Somerset House, was a floating place of entertainment, like the *Caledonia,* the *Hispaniola* or, in a different context, the *Wellington,* hall today of the Master Mariners' Company. Boulton, writing in *Amusements of Old London* vol. 2 (190), commented: 'Until our own times its value as a highway was recognised to the full, so much so, that even as late as the Regency, it was computed that the number of Wherries on the Thames exceeded that of Hackney coaches on the streets by many thousands'. After 1856 the city livery companies sold their barges, sometimes for as little as £75 or £100. When, in 1973, it was decided by the Corporation that tourists should be encouraged to visit St Paul's Cathedral by water rather than by road, it was significant that some of the companies were already considering the possibility of commissioning a livery barge again, and Dr Adam Fox, in his *Brief History of the Skinners' Company,* had advocated a dignified motor boat for guild use, a custom in Venice today. The 1953 Thames Pageant showed the guilds could, and should, lead the way in reviving William Blake's *Chartered Thames* as a colourful highway of tradition, sport and traffic-reducing commerce.

THE COMPANIES

This section is a preamble to the individual short entries devoted to each company. The following factors must be borne in mind when considering any particular company.

The companies could be listed alphabetically, in groups of appropriate trades, or in order of precedence. Alphabetical order has been selected as being more convenient for readers who may not be familiar with the City of London, but precedence is important. The official number of each company was 'sette, ordeyned and agreed' by an act of the Court of Aldermen in 1515 starting with the Mercers and the twelve Great companies and proceeding through the seventy or so minor companies. The number of each company is shown in brackets after the name. One amusing battle of precedence concerned the sixth place. The Skinners and Merchant Taylors were disputing this, and the Mayor in 1484, Billesden, decreed the Skinners to be sixth next year and the Merchant Taylors seventh and the following year to change places and so on every year, except if the Mayor should be of one of the companies, whereupon that company took precedence. It is said that from this came the phrase 'at sixes and sevens'. There have of course been other disputes between livery companies during past centuries.

Livery halls are private property and cannot be entered any more than other halls except on the annual open days, details of which can be obtained from the Corporation of London Information Bureau.

Official colours of the guilds appear at the end of the sections and have been provided by Ede and Ravenscroft Ltd. of Chancery Lane, robe-makers and tailors from 1689, and royal warrant holders.

Also listed at the end of each section is the standard reference book on that company. Some of these will be out of print or privately printed, and copies can therefore only be consulted in libraries like Guildhall and in some cases London Library.

Details have not been given of the charities administered by all the livery companies, as charity accounts are lodged with the Charity Commissioners.

All the companies have plate, consisting of cups, staves, dishes, basins, and particularly loving cups. After a dinner, instead of taking wine, a loving cup will pass down each sprig. As your neighbour, say on the left, takes part in the ceremony you rise and stand with your back to him or her. At the right moment you turn around to find him facing you holding in both hands the handles of the cup: you bow, then with your right or dagger hand you lift the cover from the cup whilst he drinks; his neighbour on the other side still standing back to back with him, he wipes the cup with the napkin attached to one handle; you replace the cover, bow, take the cup from him with both hands and turn to face your right-hand neighbour. Your left-hand neighbour turns his back to you while your right-hand neighbour repeats the ritual by taking the cover of the cup in his right hand so that you may drink without fear of being struck down; not more than three persons stand at one time. Allegedly, the sixteen-year-old King Edward was stabbed in the back in 978, by order of his stepmother, Elfrida, whilst drinking a cup of wine she offered him at the gate of Corfe Castle. The ceremony was known in Anglo-Saxon times.

Only the companies still in existence are dealt with here, but there have been many others, some of which have been absorbed into other companies and others that have died away, including the Starch-makers, Hatband-makers, Pursers, Galoche-makers, Virginals-makers and Heaumers.

At different times various ordinances have been passed, rather on the lines of consumer protection, affecting the goods or services, preventing mixing old furs with new, stinking fish, extracting dough through holes in the tables of rival bakers and so on; the punishments were unpleasant!

Many of the livery companies have severed completely their connections with the trade in their name, other than perhaps donations to the appropriate trade charities, but some, like the Goldsmiths' and Fishmongers' companies, exercise functions as extensive as those of six centuries ago. Others, like the Apothecaries' and Spectacle Makers', issue degrees to practice and some, like the Air Pilots and Air Navigators', Master Mariners' and Brewers', insist on trade connections and qualifications on all entrants; still more have in their ranks members of their trade, which the company supports by, for example, scholarships, prizes and awards.

Freemen of the City of London may join the Guild of Freemen and there is an unusual club for liverymen only, the City Livery Club, situated on Blackfriars Embankment in the historic theological college, Sion College. The club was founded in 1914 at a time when there was talk of a club for freemen and of a livery hall (not to be confused with the one now in Guildhall) for those livery companies without a hall of their own; it is perhaps significant that, in the last list of members (1972), of approximately three thousand members of the sixteen thousand liverymen in all companies, only 134 belonged to the twelve great companies. The City Livery Club has wide and extremely active sports sections, a remarkably varied and attractive social diary and on its trips in Britain and abroad is universally received with the respect given to visiting governments or official visitors.

One day in the year when all liverymen may be seen together other than on the Quarter Day or extra-ordinary Common Hall is the United Guilds Service at St Paul's Cathedral, attended by the Lord Mayor and his two sheriffs.

The ward clubs are entirely separate to the livery companies, and as their name implies are strong, active social organisations representing the electors in a city ward.

Members of royalty for the last five hundred years have been happy to belong to the city livery companies. Kings and princes have become members of the livery and queens, princesses and duchesses have become free women or free sisters of the companies.

For example, in 1885-86 His Royal Highness the Duke of Clarence and Avondale became a member of the Fishmongers', Goldsmiths' and Mercers' Companies. The Saddlers' Company

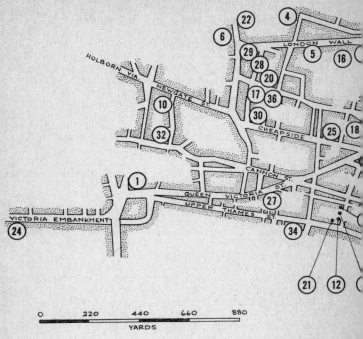

1. Apothecaries
2. Armourers
3. Bakers
4. Barbers
5. Brewers
6. Butchers
7. Carpenters
8. Clothworkers
9. Coopers
10. Cutlers

11. Drapers
12. Dyers
13. Fanmakers
14. Fishmongers
15. Founders
16. Girdlers
17. Goldsmiths
18. Grocers
19. Gunmakers

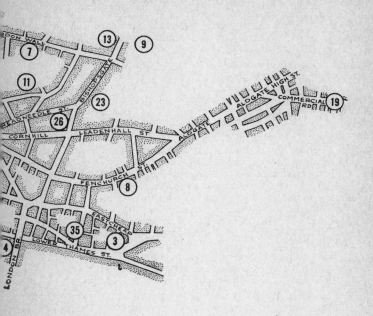

LONDON COMPANIES

20. Haberdashers
21. Innholders
22. Ironmongers
23. Leathersellers
24. Master Mariners
25. Mercers
26. Merchant Taylors
27. Painter-Stainers
28. Pewterers

29. Plaisterers
30. Saddlers
31. Skinners
32. Stationers and Newspaper Makers
33. Tallow Chandlers
34. Vintners
35. Watermen and Lightermen
36. Wax Chandlers

17

had Frederick, Prince of Wales, as freeman in 1736 and in 1909 the Duke of Connaught as Royal Perpetual Master. In 1932 the then Prince of Wales, later the Duke of Windsor, received, as first master, the Grant of Livery for the Master Mariners, Air Pilots and Air Navigators, and became a member of the City Livery Club.

The halls of the companies have from time to time been used for national events, including during the General Strike: Fishmongers' Hall was used as a British Restaurant during the Second World War; lotteries were drawn at Coopers' hall in 1809; and August 1717 saw the foundation of what was later called the Royal Exchange Assurance Company, the Mercers' Hall Marine Company.

Most companies have several charters and occasionally one is referred to as the Charter of Incorporation. The meaning of this is that the early chartered corporations were legally corporations even without the attributes that later became the hallmark of corporate status. *Halsbury's Laws of England* (third edition, 1954, vol. 9) states that no special words are required for incorporation to be inferred and additionally that a town's inhabitants were incorporated if they were granted a guild by the king, a footnote indicating a grant to 'successors' was a distinguishing feature. Later on in the same volume it is clear that the first charters of incorporation were granted by King Edward III to livery companies.

Guilds have always been connected with music and drama from the waits and pageants to the enactment of biblical or allegorical scenes in mystery plays and processions. In some towns the Carpenters, for example, would enact Noah and the Ark on their cart, just as today in British and continental carnival processions different societies have their own floats with colourful scenes. An unusual connection told by Donald Rumbelow, police historian and author, is the street ballad, like this example from Lord Mayor Sir John Cowan, Bt., 1837, Wax Chandler, to the new queen:

> *Wick*toria, all hail! may thy bonny blue eye
> Ne'er with tears of dull sorrow be *dripping,*
> May the *stores* all increase, and thy country's *mould*
> For ever in riches be *dipping.*

> May you never *wax* warm in debate, my dear Queen,
> Nor care a *rush-light* for the faction;
> For they who'd oppose thy wise councils, I ween,
> Are *taper* in thought and in action.

Punch in the 1840s enquired why Lord Mayors, like Sir Peter Laurie, Bt., 1832, needed seven trumpeters 'whose united efforts could not have blown his trumpet for him half so well as he blows his own—for nothing!'

Thomas Hood in his 'Ode for the 9th November' said:

> 'O Lud, I say,
> Was there no better day
> To fix on, than Nov 9 so shivery
> And dull for showing the Livery's Livery?
> Dimming, alas!
> The Brazier's brass,
> Soiling th'Embroiders and all the Saddlers,
> Sopping the Furriers,
> Draggling the Curriers,
> And making Merchant Tailors dirty paddlers:
> Drenching the Skinners' Company to the skin,
> Making the crusty Vintner chiller,
> And turning the Distiller
> To cold without instead of warm within;—
> Spoiling the bran-new beavers
> Of Waxchandlers and Weavers,
> Plastering the Plasterers and spotting Mercers,
> Hearty November-cursers—
> And showing Cordwainers and dapper Drapers
> Sadly in want of brushes and of scrapers;
> Making the Grocers' Company not fit
> For Company a bit;
> Dying the Dyers with a dingy flood,
> Daubing incorporated Bakers,
> And leading the Patten-makers,
> Over their very pattens in the mud,—
> O Lud! O Lud! O Lud!'

Air Pilots and Air Navigators (81)

The Guild of Air Pilots and Air Navigators was established in 1929 and became a livery company on 11th July 1956. An upper freeman, a freeman or a cadet must be an air pilot or air navigator, or a full-time student, and members of the services and glider pilots are eligible for consideration; admission to the livery is always an honour to recognise achievement. For thirty-six years, until 1968, the guild's panel of examiners was responsible for the issue of certificates of competence to flyers. The guild gives wide and varied assistance to its members, in the City tradition and not as a trade union, awards various prizes, and is honoured with various responsibilities by government departments.

The Patron is the Queen, the Grand Master is the Duke of Edinburgh. The livery includes many famous names in aviation, including Sir Thomas Sopwith, and not only is there at least one woman member of the livery but the guild has a woman secretary.

The guild is unique in having a branch in Australia and publishes a private history.

Colours: blue and cerise.

Society of Apothecaries (58)

After seceding from the Grocers the Apothecaries received their first charter in 1617 and have been a craft guild from foundation, all the original members being engaged in the art and mystery. The society gradually developed into a medical licensing body granting the degree of LMSSA, post-graduate diplomas, and after the passing of the 1815 Apothecaries Act the granting of a dispenser's certificate. The many distinguished members included Gideon Delaune, a founder and the apothecary to Anne of Denmark, John Parkinson who was royal apothecary to James I, John Keats (1795-1821) who qualified with distinction and practised for a year before becoming a poet, and the 'father of British neurology', John Hughlings Jackson (1835-1911). In 1673 the society founded the Chelsea Physic Garden of four acres and handed it over in 1899 to the trustees of London Parochial Charities.

The hall is situated in Blackfriars Lane, EC4, on a little cobbled street, and was rebuilt after the Great Fire of London between 1668 and 1670.

The society has a collection of British and foreign pharmacy, porcelain and stoneware.

Book: *Apothecaries of London;* Dr W. S. C. Copeman; 1967.

Colours: yellow and blue.

Armourers and Brasiers (22)

Originally the Guild of St George of the Armourers dating from 25th January 1322, the company still possesses its principal charters dating from 1453, 1559, 1685 and 1708, the latter incorporating the Brasiers with the Armourers. It was totally engaged in its craft on formation, providing service, assistance and hospitality both to its own fraternity and the community, and these aims are still carried out though the trade of an armourer no longer exists. The company maintains a collection of armour and weapons including the tilting suit of Sir Henry Leigh KG, Queen Elizabeth's champion from 1559 to 1599. The company provides funds for research fellowships in metallurgy at various universities. The City of London Yeomanry (Rough Riders), formed in 1900, was affiliated to the company from 1938 to 1961 when it amalgamated with the Inns of Court Regiment and the affiliation continues with the amalgamated regiment. In 1973 the company entered into its first property venture outside London at Bristol.

The hall is at 81 Coleman Street, EC2; the site of the Dragon and Two Shoppes was leased in 1346, and purchased in 1428; surviving the Great Fire, it was pulled down 1840, rebuilt and fortunately escaped the blitz on London.

Book: *An Introduction to the Worshipful Company of Armourers and Brasiers*; Rear Admiral R. S. Foster-Brown CB (printed privately).

Colours: white and black; yellow and blue.

Bakers (19)

That there was a fraternity of bakers as early as 1155 is borne out by payments to the exchequer, but the company's charters are dated 1486, 1569 and 1685. Control over the craft was exercised by Assize of Bread until the end of the eighteenth century and although the monopoly of the white and brown bakers was protected, their output was subject to strong scrutiny; the bakers' dozen (thirteen) was an insurance against short weight. In 1252 they were forbidden to put the cross or *Agnus Dei* on bread though today the cross is regularly shown on hot cross buns. The early payments to the Exchequer, probably for the removal of tolls, was in connection with 'hallmoot' which the bakers themselves controlled for some years before the City took it over.

After having their first hall in Dowgate for sixteen years, a hall was built in Harp Lane and destroyed in the Great Fire of 1666. It was rebuilt ten years later only to be burnt down in 1715 and was again rebuilt, between 1719 and 1722, and destroyed a third time in 1940; the present hall was rebuilt and opened in 1963.

Book: *A Short History of the Worshipful Company of Bakers of London*; Sylvia Thrupp; 1933.

Colours: blue and red.

Barbers (17)

The first recorded Master of the Fraternity of Barbers was Richard le Barber in 1308. In 1388 the return made to the writ of Richard II stated that the company had ordinances made of the time 'to which the memory reneweth not'. The earliest charter was granted by Edward IV in 1462. Acts of Parliament of 1540 joined, and of 1745 separated, the Barbers and Surgeons. In 1163 Pope Alexander III forbade clergy practising surgery. The company kept a stern eye on professional practices, forbade advertising, and Sunday trading, and founded an anatomical theatre. The outstanding Master was Thomas Vicary in 1530, 1546, 1548 and 1557; he was also Sergeant-Surgeon to Henry VIII, Edward VI, Mary I and Elizabeth I. The present-day barber's pole, one of the few surviving trade signs, represents the wand used in vene-section, the two bandages and the barber's blood-letting dish. Five members have served as Lord Mayor. The Barber-Surgeons' hall stood in Monkwell Street, the Inigo Jones building escaping the Great Fire. The Queen Mother opened the fourth and present hall in Monkwell Square in 1968 to make a charming oasis in the Barbican's amorphous expanse. Built on a lower level, now flanked by the Roman wall and a planned physic garden, it will display the foundations of the bastion outside the livery hall, which houses the famous Holbein painting of the king symbolically handing a charter to the Master of the United Company. Other paintings include a portrait of the Duchess of Richmond by Sir Peter Lely. The company's treasures include gifts from Henry VIII, Charles II and Queen Anne, together with a screen formerly thought to have been given gratefully by William Duell, who was hanged at Tyburn for rape on 24th November 1740. He was brought for dissection to Surgeons' Hall, but he recovered and was later transported. (The story was denied in the annals.)

Book: *Annals of the Barber Surgeons' Company;* Sidney Young; 1890; *The Vicary Lecture 1969*; R. Theodore Beck; reprinted 1970.

Colours: white and black.

Basketmakers (52)

This company was constituted by the Court of Aldermen in 1569, granted a livery of thirty in 1825 (now standing at four hundred) and received its charter from George VI in 1937. The senior officer is not known as the master, but as the Prime Warden, formerly the Upper Warden. The company was formed to regulate and control the basketmaking trade in the City of London, and by an order of Common Council of 12th October 1463 (3 Edw 4) trade had concentrated in the manor of Blanche Appleton, in the area of the present Guild Church. The company possesses not only a superb collection, extending more than three centuries, of plate, regalia and records, but many examples of basketwork, including some miniature Madeira baskets, presented by the late Princess Royal when she became an honorary freewoman, as was the late Queen Mary.

Book: *The Basketmakers' Company;* Bobart and Perrin (privately issued).

Colours: white and blue.

Blacksmiths (40)

Saint Eloy or Eloi, or Loye, was the patron saint of the Blacksmiths not only in the fourteenth-century fraternity but right up to the Reformation. The main charters were in 1571, 1604 and 1639 and until about 1783 their control of the craft was complete, not excluding the drawing of teeth and the making of spurs, the Spurriers having been amalgamated with them in 1571.

The company had a hall in Lambeth Hill in Castle Baynard Ward from 1494 until the outbreak of the Great Fire and it was rebuilt in 1671. The company's lease of its hall from the City corporation terminated in 1785.

Book: *History of the Worshipful Company of Blacksmiths;* Arthur Adams; 1951.

Colours: yellow and black.

Bowyers (38)

The Bowyers, or makers of bows, received their Grant of Arms on 20th November 1488, but they were certainly recognised in 1371 when the Fletchers and Bowmen petitioned for the union between the two crafts to be broken, the Bowyers petitioning for no night work because of the risk of inferior workmanship. Their charter was received on 25th May 1621 and regranted on 17th November 1666/1670. Before the days of gunpowder, archery was of vital importance to the country's defence and the practising at different times has been compulsory; the company still encourages archery and shooting. Unlike other companies, the Master serves a two-year term, and one outstanding Master was R. J. B. Neville, MA (1972-1974). The company's motto is 'Crécy, Poitiers, Agincourt', from the three battles (respectively 1346, 1356, and 1415) when the day was carried by longbowmen (draw-weight 100lb, drawn to the ear, not just to the breast as with shortbowmen).

Alderman Finnis, a Bowyer, was the last Lord Mayor to have his procession on the Thames (1856).

Until 1666 the hall stood at the corner of Hart Street and Monkwell Street.

Colours: white and black.

Brewers (14)

The Brewers' conditions of membership are as strict today as they were in 1437, when they received from Henry II the first of eight charters, the last dated 1685. Their patron saint was St Thomas a Becket. They controlled the brewing of ale, both the quality of the product and the workers in the trade, in the City and suburbs. Their minute books date from 1418 and include the company dispute with Lord Mayor Richard Whityngton because the company 'had fat swans at their feast on the morrow of St Martins when he had none at his'.

Today members must be directors of brewery companies operating within a seven-mile radius of the City or with substantial trading interests in the area. The company are estate governors to Aldenham School in Hertfordshire and the Dame Alice Owen School, now in Islington but moving to Potters Bar.

Humphrey Parsons was Master in 1730 and served twice as Lord Mayor of London.

The company had land in Addle Street in 1291 and its first hall certainly dated from 1418, being burnt down in the Great Fire. The second hall, completed in 1673, was destroyed in 1940 and the present hall, in Aldermanbury Square, was completed in 1960.

Book: *A Short History of the Worshipful Company of Brewers;* 1932 (out of print).

Colours: white and red.

Broderers (48)

'Oh! give us your plain dealing fellows
Who never from honesty shrink.'

So starts the Master's song believed to be unique in the

24

City. The Oxford Dictionary has a reference to two Brouderers in 1376; the tapicers or tapissers of 1331 (already mentioned in the extract from *Canterbury Tales*) appear to have been absorbed by the Broderers who were referred to as the company in 1430-31. The charter granted by Queen Elizabeth in 1561 was destroyed in the Second World War; other charters are dated 1609 to 1686 and the control of the trade or mystery (French: *metier*) of embroidery was very extensive in London. Today the company assists in maintaining an apprentice at the Royal College of Needlework. The company possesses its Grant of Arms dated 17th August 1558.

The Broderers, like the Masons and Cooks, have been associated with the Mercers for more than 340 years.

Two broderers, Sir Walter Wilkins (1895), and Sir Robert Bellinger (1966; Master, 1963) have been Lord Mayor.

The company's hall in Gutter Lane, rebuilt in the nineteenth century to suit the requirements of Messrs. Morley, the Manchester warehousemen, was destroyed in 1940 and the site sold in 1957.

Book: *A Chat about the Broderers' Company;* Christopher Holford (Past Master); 1910 (out of print).

Colours: white and blue.

Butchers (24)

As early as A.D. 975 there was a hall for butchers outside the City walls, and in 1179 there is a reference to the Guild of Butchers in the Pipe Roll. The charters date from 1605 and 1637 and the guild controlled both the killing and selling of meat, including even their right to slaughter cattle in the City. Today the company maintains direct contact with the meat and live trade.

Daniel Defoe was admitted to the freedom of the company.

In 1548 the company's hall was in the Newgate Flesh Market; destroyed in 1666, it was built on the Pudding Lane site in 1667 and given up about 1884. In 1884-85 the new hall was built at 87 Bartholomew Close, EC1, only to be seriously damaged by bombs in 1944 and rebuilt in 1960. One of its most striking features is a magnificent huge tapestry showing the development of the guild and trade.

Book: *The Worshipful Company of Butchers;* 1962.

Colours: white and blue.

Carmen (77)

In 1516 the Fraternity of St Katherine the Virgin and Martyr was formed to give the Carmen a monopoly of plying for hire in the City in return for moving the royal household whenever required, thus deterring the king from helping himself!

The fixing of rates, licensing of vehicles, siting of stands and prevention of disputes were fraught with problems. For some time the Carmen were under the governor of Christ's Hospital and for years the Woodmongers and Carmen were incorporated together. In 1668, the Carmen became an independent fellowship by act of Common Council, procured a similar act in 1830, their charter from King George VI in 1946, and in 1953 were permitted to increase their livery to 450. All licensed carters must be freemen of the company.

Book: *The Worshipful Company of Carmen;* Eric Bennett; 1952.

Colours: white and red.

Carpenters (26)

Before the Great Fire, Carpenters were paramount in the building trade, and their fraternity certainly dates from 1333. Charters were granted in 1477, 1558, 1560, 1607, 1674 and 1686; the company controlled the craft with religious and charitable aims. After the Fire, London was mainly rebuilt in brick, but, interestingly, the hall escaped the conflagration and was let to several Lord Mayors during the rebuilding of their own mansions, so now each newly elected Lord Mayor dines at the hall. The officers are crowned with the original 1561 crowns, and using the four early seventeenth-century steeple cups. The Queen of the Netherlands and Field Marshal Viscount Montgomery have been awarded the freedom. The Carpenters are unique in having an offshoot in America, in the Carpenters' Company of the City and County of Philadelphia, dating from 1724, President and Master being honorary members of each other's company. The Master for 1973-74 was Osbert Lancaster, CBE. Seven Carpenters have served as Lord Mayor.

The hall dated from 1429, with additions from 1550 and 1664, but the new hall, built from 1876 to 1880 when Throgmorton Avenue was constructed, was gutted on 10th and 11th May 1941, to be reopened in 1960; it shows the craft of carpentry to great advantage.

Books: *Historical Account of the Worshipful Company of*

Carpenters; E. B. Jupp, W. W. Pocock; 1887. *A History of the Carpenters' Company;* B. W. E. Alford and T. C. Barker; 1968.

Colours: white and black.

Clockmakers (61)

Originally part of the Blacksmiths, the company received its charter in 1631, and by 1637 the Clockmakers free of the company had to bind their apprentices to a warden. The horological trade in the City and ten miles around was controlled, and as in other English and Continental companies, a masterpiece or proof-piece had to be submitted before a member was admitted.

The company's magnificent collection of clocks and watches is displayed at Guildhall Library, and it owns an extensive library of books, documents and portraits.

Outstanding masters include Thomas Tompion (1702), B. L. Vulliamy (1821) and John Grant (1838); both of the latter on five occasions.

Three members have served as Lord Mayor.

Book: *Some Account of the Worshipful Company of Clockmakers;* Aikens and Overall, 1881 (out of print).

Colours: yellow and black.

Clothworkers (12)

The amalgamation of the Fullers, incorporated 1480 and listed in 1376, and the Shearmen, incorporated 1508 and listed 1350, produced the Clothworkers' company, known as the Guild or Fraternity of the Assumption of the Blessed Virgin Mary of Clothworkers, receiving its charter from Henry VIII on 18th January 1528. It was to play a strong role protecting the interests of the craft, not least in withstanding Elizabeth's habit of granting of patents, in this case to Edward Darcy, at the close of the sixteenth century. One outstanding Master was Samuel Pepys, who lived near the hall and was elected to the freedom, livery, and the master's chair in 1677, at the height of his power, aged forty-four. Present-day support to the trade includes that given to the Departments of Textile Industries and Colour Chemistry and Dyeing, known as the Clothworkers' Department, at Leeds University. Many clothworkers have served as Lord Mayor.

The site of the hall, in Dunster Court, Mincing Lane,

was purchased by the Shearmen in 1456, and is the sixth on the site; it was opened in April 1958 by the late Princess Royal, an Honorary Freewoman, as was the late Princess Marina, Duchess of Kent, who laid the foundation stone two years earlier.

Book: *The Golden Ram. A Narrative History of the Clothworkers' Company*, 1528-1958; Thomas Girtin; 1958 (privately printed).

Colours: white and black.

Coachmakers and Coach Harnessmakers (72)

With charters in 1677 and 1687 the company originally controlled its trade completely, whilst feasible, until 1804, but active trade participation ended in the First World War. Today it allots trade design prizes for the motor industry. Lionel Lukin, the inventor of the lifeboat, was Master in 1793, and Prince Arthur of Connaught in 1932; in 1867 the then Duke of Edinburgh opened the new hall and became a member of the Court.

At Lord Derby's inquiry in 1883 the company proved that seventy of the livery of 120 were connected with the trade and nineteen of the Court of 27 were master coach-builders or otherwise connected with the craft.

Today's six-a-side railway coach is based on stage-coach seating.

Sir Walter Wilkin was Lord Mayor in 1895.

The company hall was the base in 1780 of meetings leading to the Gordon Riots; it was rebuilt in 1870 and later destroyed.

Book: *A History of the Worshipful Company of Coach Makers and Coach Harnessmakers of London;* G. Eland; 1937.

Colours: yellow and blue.

Cooks (35)

The first cook's shop, in Cookes Row, was described in 1170, and the fraternity dates from 1311 and 1312. Thereafter till 1438 there are references to the masters of the misteries of Cooks, Pastelers and Piebakers, later amalgamated into the Cooks of East Cheap and Bread Street. The first grant of arms was in 1461 and the first charter in 1482; later charters were between 1519 and 1939. The guild regulated and assisted the trade and crafts of cooking and catering in the City and provided charity for cooks. The company has been in association with the Mercers, Masons and Broderers for 340 years.

Outstanding Masters include Peter Romilly in 1761, father of Sir Samuel and grandfather of the first Lord Romilly, eminent lawyers, and Samuel Birch, leading City caterer, in 1799. Samuel Birch was Lord Mayor in 1814-15.

The company had a hall in Aldersgate Street from 1500 until 1771, and still owns the site.

Book: *The Cook's Company—Short History;* F. Taverner; Philips, 1966.

Colours: white and red.

Coopers (36)

The Coopers, or makers of barrels, existed before 1396 and their five charters date between 1501 and 1685. A religious organisation, with the right to use the communal hall at burials and payment for masses, gradually developed into a trade organisation, controlling the industry, which changed during the years. In the nineteenth century the company revived the custom of selecting the Master from the Court but the wardens from the livery, so that after their year of office they returned to the livery to await their election to the Court. Sir John Fleet, 1692, Sir David Salamans, 1855, Sir Alfred James Newton, 1899, and Sir Robert Wilmot, 1742, served as Lord Mayor, the last being the first to refuse to be translated to one of the major twelve companies.

The company had a hall in Basinghall Street from 1547 until 1666; rebuilt in 1670 it was pulled down in 1865, rebuilt 1869 and destroyed in 1940. The hall was used for the last state lottery in 1836 and in 1809 an aquatint of the scene by Pugin and Rowlandson was included in Ackermann's *The Microcosm of London.* The present hall at 13 Devonshire Square, EC2, contains the offices and a small hall used for court meetings.

Book: *A Short History of the Worshipful Company of Coopers of London;* Sir William Foster, CIE; 1961.

Colours: yellow and red, or red and black.

Cordwainers (27)

Cordwainers, or workers in Cordoba leather, gave their name to the Ward of Cordwainer—an additional proof that workers in a craft congregate together. The first ordinances were granted in 1272 and the charters date from 1439 to 1685 and the grant of arms from 1579; the craft controlled not only shoemaking but the making of leather bottles and other goods including horse harnesses. St Crispin was the patron saint of shoemakers. An item of interest concerning the company sending goods to Virginia was furnished by a letter to the company from John Smith (1580-1631) who was saved from the Indians by Pocahontas. He presented to the company a copy of his *History of Virginia*.

The building first used as a hall in 1393, rebuilt 1577, destroyed 1666, rebuilt again in 1670, 1788 and 1910, and was destroyed in 1941, breaking a continuity of five centuries on the same site at 7 Cannon Street.

Book: *A Descriptive and Historical Account of the Cordwainers of the City of London;* C. H. Waterland Mander; 1931.

Colours: yellow and blue.

Curriers (29)

The Curriers, who dress the leather for further treatment, were originally part of the Cordwainers with whom they were in dispute for many years. They had a fraternity in the Priory of the Carmelites by 1389, and the ordinances still extant date from 1415. The governing charter is dated 1605, and their originally complete control of the craft lasted until 1852, when the *List of Curriers' Prices* was ordered *not* to be reprinted. The company maintained a connection by annual grants to the Cordwainers' technical college.

A craftsman named Thomas Sterne gave the company a property in Cripplegate for its first hall. In all, six halls have stood on this site but the last was sold in 1922 and destroyed in 1941.

Book: *The Curriers and the City of London;* Edward Mayer; 1968.

Colours: yellow and blue.

Cutlers (18)

The Cutlers existed in 1389; their charter dates from 1416 and their grant of arms from 1476. They were powerful enough to give out work to other crafts like the Sheathers and Blademakers, although their original control over the craft had died away by the mid-eighteenth century. Their work encompassed not only the making of swords but also of surgical instruments, and today the company fosters apprenticeships to leading instrument manufacturers.

Several Masters and Senior Wardens have served as Lord Mayor, the latest being Lord Mais of Walbrook in 1972-73.

The company had had four halls on different sites between 1285 and 1882 when extensions to the District Railway Company caused them to move to Warwick Lane, EC4, where the fifth hall was built in 1887, damaged in 1941 and restored.

Books: *History of the Cutlers' Company of London;* Charles Welch; 1923. *A Brief History;* Dudley Hayton; 1956.

Colours: white and red.

Distillers (69)

The Distillers, like the Brewers, are unique in restricting membership to practising distillers. Their grant of arms was received in 1638 when they also received their charter, but this was not enrolled by the City until 1658; the next charter was 1688 and a Grant of Livery 1672. They were formed to regulate the trade and manufacture of 'artificial and strong waters, and making of Beeregar and Alegar in London' and the environs. The founder, Theodore de Mayerne, who secured the charter, was physician to Henry IV of France, James I, Charles I and Charles II. In 1660 a Quaker, Robert Toone, was admitted, and three years later Anthony Haig was imprisoned in the Tolbooth in Edinburgh for four years and four months for being a Quaker; his family is even more famous today.

The company has never had a hall but rumour had it that one was destroyed in 1666.

Colours: white and blue.

Drapers (3)

The highly important merchants in woollen cloth had an association in the twelfth century: the first royal charter was granted by Edward III in 1364, later charters being granted in 1438 and 1466: the grant of a coat of arms in 1439 is the earliest surviving to a corporate body. The influence of Drapers in civic and national affairs became immeasurable and today the Drapers' Company is a mighty and efficient charitable body to which many educational, medical and

31

artistic organisations owe more than is generally realised; in 1959 the Drapers' Charitable Fund was established.

The list of Drapers serving as Lord Mayors, sheriffs, aldermen and MPs is immense; in early years many drapers served more than one period, two examples being Ralph Hardel, 1254-1259, and Elias Russell, 1299-1301. The mighty John of Northampton, one of the most impressive and powerful figures in London history, was Mayor in 1381-82 and 1382-83.

The first hall (1424-26) was in St Swithin's Lane, the present site in Throgmorton Street being purchased from Henry VIII in 1543; it was destroyed in 1666, rebuilt six years later, and has been altered and redecorated on subsequent occasions. It contains many works of art ranging from furniture and carpets to paintings, including portraits of the royal family and Lord Nelson, a member of the company. The hall stands round a courtyard and has a charming garden containing mulberry trees whose predecessors go back three centuries.

Books: *The Triple Crowns;* Tom Girtin. *The History of the Worshipful Company of the Drapers of London;* Reverend A. H. Johnson.

Colours: yellow and blue.

Dyers (13)

The Dyers were incorporated to establish a ' Fraternity of perpetual Guild in London and the suburbs, to the praise, glory and honour of Almighty God and of the most glorious Virgin Mary ' and ' To oversee, rule and govern ' the trade of dyeing; the first charter was dated 1471 and the ninth and last, 1704. The company has the privilege of a royalty of a game of swans on the Thames, shared only with the Queen and the Vintners, whose records first make mention of the Dyers' royalty in 1609. Around this time it was ruled that dyers free of other companies had to swear the oath for true dyeing although they were not forced to bind their apprentices at Dyers' Hall.

Sir Cuthbert Hackett served as Lord Mayor in 1626 after he was translated, as was then customary, to the Drapers' company.

It is supposed that the original hall was in Anchor Lane c. 1480, the next two being at the Three Stars further east in Upper Thames Street, and three more halls being on the present site in Dowgate Hill. The present hall was built in

1. *The Lord Mayor's Coach and the famous Whitbread Shire horses. These magnificent horses are frequently used in all aspects of London pageantry.*

2. *'The procession with Cleopatra's Needle passing down Gracechurch Street' on the Lord Mayor's Day 1877, as seen in 'The Graphic'.*

3. *The Masters of the Guilds in full livery process into Common Hall (Guildhall, 1973). The Master of the author's mother company, the Poulters, is shown bottom right.*

4. In the Small Court Room at Mercers' Hall, a Liveryman in gown and hood is attended by a waiter in the Mercers' Staff Livery including the special gilt buttons.

5. *The Apothecaries' Hall in Blackfriars Lane on a little cobbled street; it was rebuilt between 1668 and 1670 after the Great Fire of London.*

6. *The arms and supporters of the Armourers and Braziers on the roof of the Hall in Coleman Street, E.C.2. The Company maintains a collection of armour and weapons.*

7. The Fishmongers' Hall seen from the new London Bridge. The most outstanding Master was Sir William Walworth in 1381; in the same year he slew Wat Tyler, the leader of the mob burning and plundering London.

8. *The Proof House of the Gunmakers' Company in Commercial Road.*

9. *The 'Wellington' has been the Livery Hall of the Master Mariners since it was acquired from the Admiralty in 1947.*

10. *The new Plaisterers' Hall opened in 1970 against the original London Wall.*

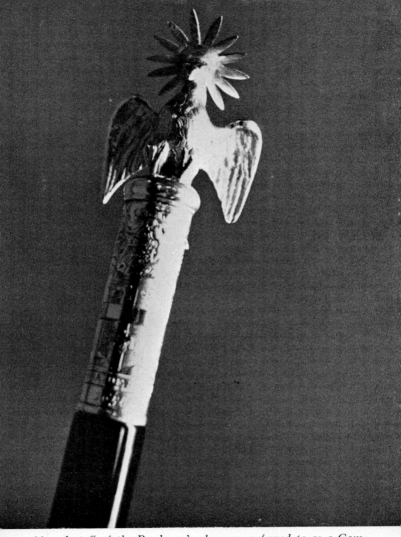

11. *A staff of the Broderers' who were referred to as a Com-*
pany in 1430-31.

12. *The funeral pall of the Saddlers' Company showing,
below, the decoration sewn over the image of the Virgin;
note the defacement of the Virgin's head.*

13. *The unique ballot box of the Saddlers' Company showing the short funnel hiding the movement of a cuffed
hand dropping an election ball into one of the three
boxes below.*

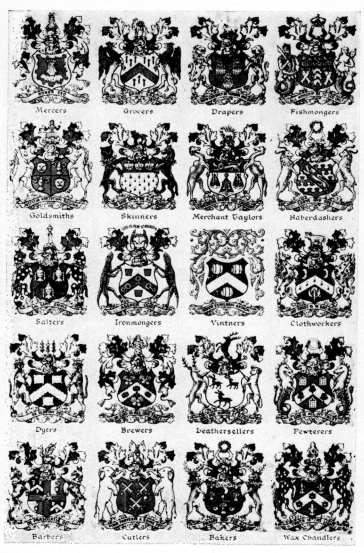

14.   *The coats of arms of the London Companies.*

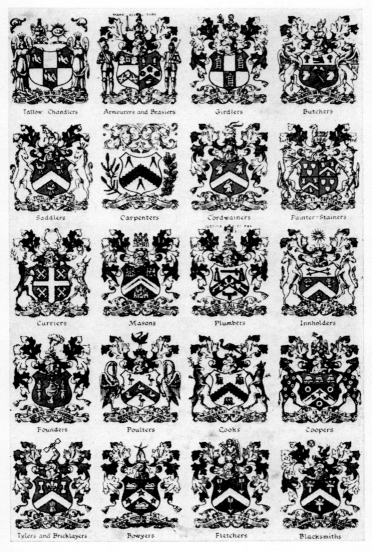

Tallow Chandlers   Armourers and Brasiers   Girdlers   Butchers

Saddlers   Carpenters   Cordwainers   Painter-Stainers

Curriers   Masons   Plumbers   Innholders

Founders   Poulters   Cooks   Coopers

Tylers and Bricklayers   Bowyers   Fletchers   Blacksmiths

15.   *The coats of arms of the London Companies.*

Joiners Weavers Woolmen Scriveners

Fruiterers Plaisterers Stationers and Newspaper Makers Broderers

Upholders Musicians Turners Basketmakers

Glaziers Horners Farriers Paviors

Loriners Apothecaries Shipwrights Spectacle Makers

16. *The coats of arms of the London Companies.*

Clockmakers Glovers Feltmakers Framework Knitters

Needlemakers Gardeners Tinplate Workers Wheelwrights

Distillers Pattenmakers Glass Sellers Coachmakers

Gunmakers Gold & Silver Wyre Drawers Makers of Playing Cards Fanmakers

Carmen Master Mariners Solicitors

17. *The coats of arms of the London Companies.*

Air Pilots & Air Navigators

Farmers

Tobacco Pipe Makers
and Tobacco Blenders

Furniture Makers

Scientific Instrument
Makers

18. *The coats of arms of the London Companies.*

19. *The stage waterman takes leave of his oars, coat and badge, drawn by George Cruikshank (George Cruikshank's Table Book, 1845).*

1840 and contains many items of interest including an illuminated window designed by Laurence Whistler, paintings, furniture, plate and panelling; the 1578 ordinances show the arms of the company which are prior to 1530.

Book: *A Short History of the Ancient Mystery of the Dyers of the City of London;* J. N. Daynes; 1965 (privately published).

Colours: white and black.

Fanmakers (76)

The Fanmakers are the youngest of the old City guilds, having received their charter on 19th April 1709, and enrolled at Guildhall the following year, receiving their livery of sixty from the Court of Aldermen on 20th June 1809. The guild was formed to protect English fanmakers after the revocation of the Edict of Nantes in 1685 had driven many continental fanmakers to England. Today the senior warden is known as the Free Warden and the second warden as the Foreign Warden. By the end of the nineteenth century the use of ornamental fans had lapsed, but the company now numbers many of the makers of heating and ventilation fans. The company possesses a number of beautiful fans, and traditionally the members of the royal family sign a fan.

Two Masters, Sir Alfred James Newton, Bart, and Colonel Sir Charles Arthur Davis, have served as Lord Mayor respectively in 1899-1900 and 1946.

By 1944 the company had a friendly arrangement to have its 'hall' in Lime Street, the church of St Edmund the King, and it has a similar arrangement with the hall behind St Botolphs, Bishopsgate, marked by the two charity children in stone flanking the door.

Book: *A Short Account of The Worshipful Company of Fan Makers;* Bernard Ross; Collins, 1950.

Colours: yellow and red.

Farmers (80)

Surprisingly the Company of Agriculturists, later the Company of Farmers, came to birth only in 1946, as a result of the strength and co-operation built during the war effort. The livery was granted and presented on 31st October 1952, the charter on 29th July 1955, and by 1965 the permitted livery was three hundred. The company was formed to stimulate the development of agricultural education and interest in rural arts and crafts, and so has initiated advance courses in farm management. The grant of livery stipulates that the majority of the court must be persons engaged in the farming industry, and the livery includes many prominent and titled land-owners.

Colours: yellow and brown.

Farriers (55)

References to a guild occur in 1356 and in 1674 Charles II granted the charter. The aims were 'Preserving of horses by preventing their destruction by bad shoeing' and 'Increasing the number of skilful and expert farriers'. The company's responsibilities have increased during six centuries with the popularity of the horse for recreation and sports. The guild inaugurated a registration scheme for shoeing smiths in 1890 and in 1958 sponsored an apprenticeship scheme; it also holds courses and promotes competitions. Three past Masters on the Court serve as deputies on the Corporation, two having served as sheriff. The Duke of Devonshire is a past Master, and HRH the Princess Anne and the Duke of Beaufort are among the Honorary Freemen.

Books: *History of The Farriers of London to 1948;* R. C. Robson (Clerk 1942-58). *Supplementary History 1949 to 1972;* Mr Deputy L. B. Prince (past Master); 1973 (private circulation).

Colours: white and black.

Feltmakers (63)

The company's charters date from 1667, 1669 and 1772 and the livery was granted in 1733. The trade needed protection against foreign hatters, instances being recorded of 366 hats being burnt in Woolchurch Market Place and 534 foreign hats burnt in Rye. The control over the industry died away in the nineteenth century with the establishment of the trade union, simultaneously with the introduction from America of machines for felt-making. A beaver hat required rabbit fur for the body and beaver for the nap. Thanks to Queen Elizabeth I, hatters have been traditionally known as 'Gentleman Journeyman Hatters'.

Book: *History of The Worshipful Company of Feltmakers of London;* J. H. Hawkins; 1917.

Colours: white and red.

Fishmongers (4)

In these days of impersonal central government it is a welcome relief to find a livery company carrying out not only the original duties of the craft, but enhanced responsibilities recognised as the most efficient by government itself. Although a guild or society existed long before any charter, the company possesses twenty-four charters, starting with Edward I in 1272 and going on to George VI in 1937. It was formed to regulate and support the fish trade and its control was complete even to the adjudication of disputes between the public and the trade. The company possesses many statutory powers, as under the Salmon and Fresh Water Fisheries Act of 1923, the Sea Fisheries (Shell Fish) Act of 1967 and the Sea Fish (Conservation) Act 1967.

The Fishmeters still examine all fish coming into London, perhaps two hundred tons a day to Billingsgate Market, to ' Survey whether the same be wholesome for Man's body and fit to be sold or not '. Unsound fish are seized and proceedings can be initiated under the Foods and Drugs Act 1955. The company formed the Trout and Salmon Association in 1903, helped to set up the Atlantic Salmon Research Trust in 1967 and supports the Anglers Co-operative Association and the National Anglers' Council, to name only a few such bodies. The clerk is an officer of ten organisations connected with the trade. The company supports Gresham's School, founded in 1555 at Holt by Sir John Gresham, and was instrumental in setting up the City and Guilds of London Art School. Perhaps the most outstanding Master was Sir William Walworth, who in 1381 slew Wat Tyler, the leader of the mob of rebels burning and plundering London. Today Prince Philip, Duke of Edinburgh, is a member of the Court of Assistants and a past Prime Warden (the company does not have a master); the Duke of Gloucester is a freeman by patrimony; in 1971 the Prince of Wales became a freeman by patrimony and a liveryman; and in 1972 Princess Anne took up her freedom by patrimony. A number of fishmongers served as Lord Mayor up to 1862. The first hall (1310) was in a house by London Bridge and the second (1434), in the same house, was bequeathed to the company and burnt down in the Great Fire. The third hall was built in 1671 by London Bridge and demolished in 1828, three years before the new London Bridge opened. In 1834 the magnificent existing hall was opened by London Bridge, damaged in 1940, restored in 1951 and is even more impressive since the opening in 1973 of the latest London Bridge.

Treasures include the Wat Tyler dagger, and the famous Annigoni portrait of the Queen.

Colours: white and blue.

Fletchers (39)

The Fletchers, or makers of arrows, petitioned in 1371 to be separate from the Bowyers and they are a company by prescription existing from at least 1371; their aims were to ensure the quality and price of the various arrows made. They received their grant of arms in 1467. In 1363 the practice of archery at the butts was compulsory on feast days but by the 1580s the government was lamenting the decay of archery. By the end of the sixteenth century this was hastened by the use of muskets and arquebuses, although horse-archers were used in 1807 in Poland against Napoleon and the Chinese were still using bows and arrows around 1900. Today the company presents trophies to the Royal Toxophilite Society.

Three members have served as Lord Mayor, two of them in the 1960s.

The company rented a hall in St Mary-Axe at the beginning of the sixteenth century; by the eighteenth century it was let and the property was sold in 1933.

Book: *The Fletchers and Longbow String Makers of London;* Professor James E. Oxley; 1968.

Colours: yellow and blue.

Founders (33)

From the fraternity known as the Brotherhood of St Clement's, at St Lawrence Jewry, came the Founders' Company of workers in brass and brass alloys or tin-plate, known as 'latten' or 'laton', around the area still known as Lothbury. Since 1508 their parish church has been St Margaret's, Lothbury. A petition from the guild to the Lord Mayor is dated 1365 and the warden's accounts start in 1497; only three company's accounts start earlier. The charter is dated 1614. The aims were to defend the interests and standards of the founder's craft and significantly in 1973 forty-five per cent of the livery were directly connected with this craft. From 1365 to 1831 it was stipulated that all brass founders working in the City had to belong to the company. Since 1640 the retiring Master has drunk to his successor from a painted

Venetian goblet said to have been taken from Boulogne by an English archer and bequeathed to the company by Richard Weoley, Master in 1631. Two nineteenth-century Founders served as Lord Mayor. The Founders had a hall in Lothbury from 1531 until the Great Fire; it was rebuilt by the liverymen from their own funds and used to provide income. In 1845 another hall was built in Founder's Court but this was let on lease in 1853 and the company acquired its present freehold at 13 St Swithin's Lane. The freehold in Founder's Court was sold in 1964.

Books: *Annals of the Founders' Company;* W. M. Williams; 1867. *History of The Worshipful Company of Founders of the City of London;* W. N. Hibbert; 1925 (out of print).

Colours: yellow and blue.

Framework Knitters (64)

The guild is popularly supposed to have sprung into being when a master of arts of St John's College, Cambridge, named Lee, loved a country maiden more interested in knitting hose, so he devised a machine making hand-knitting unnecessary. Oxford claims a similar story except that the man had no means of supporting his wife and so invented the stocking loom to enable her to amass a fortune. Lee's descendants and their associates certainly established framework knitting in London, Godalming and Nottingham and in 1657 Oliver Cromwell granted one of the only two charters in this period to this industry. Queen Elizabeth was converted from cloth hose to silk hose by Burleigh and Leicester. Charles II gave a fresh charter in 1663 covering England and Wales and the company established subsidiary courts at Nottingham and Leicester and enjoyed a century of remarkable power, prestige and ceremony. Life became more difficult when the House of Commons felt its regulations to be in restraint of trade and a law suit in 1809 allowed anyone to set up in the industry. The company today is closely associated with the industry and a great part of the livery of 225 is actively connected with knitting and hosiery in Leicester and Nottingham. The Master's chair, dating from the seventeenth century, is kept at Guildhall Museum.

The company had an impressive hall in Red Cross Street until 1821.

Colours: white and red.

Fruiterers (45)

References to the Fruiterers occur in 1292, 1416, when a Master of Mysteries was sworn, and 1422, the Arms being on record in 1599. The charters are dated 1605-6, 1686 and 1688. In addition to fellowship and aims, the charters upheld legal rights and regulated the trade against foreign fruiterers. Today it sponsors and prints company lectures, and encourages profitable fruit-growing. It presents a gift of fruit to each Lord Mayor.

Of the Fruiterers serving as Lord Mayor, four Masters were selected between 1882 and 1904.

Book: *History of The Worshipful Company of Fruiterers of London;* Arthur William Gould; 1912.

Colours: white and green.

Furniture Makers (83)

The guild was formed in 1952, received a grant of arms two years later and was granted a livery of 250 on 29th March 1963, when the Lord Mayor was Sir Ralph Perring who had been the first Junior Warden of the Company. In early days many different crafts had been concerned with furniture making, for example Chippendale and William Vile were originally upholders. The company aims to foster the craft and design, preserving traditions, granting scholarships and accepting and creating trusts. Its membership is drawn from all aspects of designing and making furniture.

Book: *Origins and History of the Worshipful Company of Furniture Makers;* Edward H. Pinto; 1963.

Gardeners (66)

In 1345 the Gardeners petitioned the Lord Mayor to sell produce 'in front of the Church of St Austin at the side of the gate at St Paul's Churchyard'. The charters are dated 1605 and 1659 and the Grant of Livery 1891. On formation the control of the trade was complete, but by 1846 the company was in abeyance, and three generations of the Hipkin family saved it from legal extinction with its revival in the 1890s. The company's most valued privilege is to provide the Queen's bouquet at her coronation and princesses' bridal bouquets. It sponsors scholarships and the presentation of cups to horticultural societies, was prominent in the creation of St Paul's garden and its window-box scheme has done much to brighten the City.

Mr G. R. Blades (Lord Ebbisham), Master in 1912-13, was Lord Mayor in 1926-7.

Book: *The Worshipful Company of Gardeners of London —A History of its Revival 1890-1960;* Arnold F. Steele; 1964.

Colours: white and green.

Girdlers (23)

There was a fraternity of Girdlers at St Lawrence in St Lawrence Jewry in 1332 and the Girdlers received their royal charter, or letters patent, from Edward III in 1327, subsequently being granted five further charters. The company absorbed the Pinners and Wire Sellers. The girdle was an important article of clothing at one time and the company has the privilege of presenting the king at his coronation with girdle and stole, the custom being revived with George V.

In 1422-23 the Girdlers were hiring the Brewers' Hall but a decade later their own hall is listed in Bassishaw. The hall has stood on its present site in Basinghall Avenue since 1431; the hall built in 1680-87 was destroyed in 1940 and the present hall with gardens before and behind rebuilt in 1961.

Book: *The Girdlers' Company—A Second History:* Dr T. C. Baker; 1957 (printed privately).

Colours: yellow and blue.

Glass-Sellers (71)

The 1635 charter was drawn up but never enrolled, and the operative charter dates from 1664. Glass-Sellers were originally exempt from the regulation describing pedlars and chapmen as rogues and vagabonds but this became a loop-hole for all hawkers, so the Glass-Sellers were to petition in 1691 to forbid travelling Glass-Sellers as well! In the late eighteenth century there were huge imports by Glass-Sellers and there are letters listing 173 different types of glass and also explaining how to evade customs. The control of the trade declined during the nineteenth century but the charitable connections still exist. In 1951 the Glass-Sellers' company scholarship was established at Sheffield University, recalling memories of the collaboration with scientists way back in 1675, culminating in the invention by George Ravenscroft of English flint glass or lead crystal. The company made a gift of glass to the Queen for Sandringham in 1953.

Book: *The Worshipful Company of Glass-Sellers of London;* George Allan Bone; 1966.

Colours: royal blue and maroon.

Glaziers (53)

A guild existed in 1368 and the charters dated 1637 and 1685 reflect the dramatic story of English glass. Charles I granted Sir Robert Mansell the patent right to produce glass using coal but not timber as this was required for the Navy. Many glaziers objected to the quality; Inigo Jones and Thomas Baldwin stated: 'Sir R. Mansell's glass is mixed good-bad together—is very thin in the middle'. The Glaziers' first task was therefore to break the patent and to establish their own monopoly and their own trade regulations. However, English glass was in bad repute and foreign glass was preferred until 1487. An interesting story concerned the Southwark glaziers of Flemish origin, including three King's Glaziers, Barnard Flower, Galleon Hone and James Nicholson; their cash payment to the Guild enabled them to work, but when Nicholson's widow married the warden of the Guild he then possessed both halves of the agreement and was able to break it and gaol four Flemings including Hone!

Book: *History of the Worshipful Company of Glaziers . . . otherwise . . . Glaziers and Painters of Glass;* Charles Henry Ashdown; 1919.

Colours: white and black.

Glovers (62)

The Glovers of London received an ordinance in 1349 and a year later could ensure that gloves and belts of false material were 'Burnt in the High Street of Chepe'! In 1498 they were asked to join the Pursers and by 1502 were joined by ordinance to the Leathersellers. A grant of arms was made in 1464 and the charter of 1639 separated them from the Leathersellers and the 1898 charter, the only *Inspeximus* charter in Victoria's reign, confirmed their original charter. In the early days the company had the power of search but from the mid eighteenth century to the end of the nineteenth century the company was in a decline; it has been more active since 1898 and now encourages the workmanship in the trade by, for example, presentation of awards, and in 1950 one third of the livery was still in the glove trade. From the coronation of Victoria the custom began of presenting the queen with her coronation gloves.

The company had a hall in Beech Lane, Cripplegate, which was sold.

Colours: white and black.

Gold and Silver Wyre Drawers (74)

An act was passed in 1423 stating the quality of gold and silver and there is evidence of the craftsmen being banded together in fellowship by 1464. The 1623 charter was withdrawn *quo warranto* and not re-incorporated until the 1693 charter; the livery was granted in 1780. The post-revolution fashion of the late eighteenth century changed and the trade found scope in naval and military uniforms of cords and braids, and civic and ecclesiastical attire. The company still has powers of search but has not exercised them since the 1870s. An exhibition of the work and methods of the craft was held at Chelsea in 1890. All branches of the industry are represented on the court. In 1723 Mrs Christian Russell left a bequest for widows of the freemen of the company.

Book: *History of the Worshipful Company of Gold and Silver Wyre Drawers;* Horace Stewart; 1891.

Colours: yellow and blue.

Goldsmiths (5)

To this day the company has been a craft guild. 'Hallmark' means the mark applied at Goldsmiths' Hall. A fraternity of Goldsmiths existed prior to 1180; the first charter was granted in 1327. Goldsmiths were the first bankers. The company today includes prominent bankers and leading goldsmiths like Stuart Devlin. The Trial of the Pyx has taken place since 1248. The Antique Plate Committee decides disputes relating to antique gold and silver contravening hallmarking laws. The Assay Office is at the hall. The company possesses an excellent collection of gold and silver, and publishes a wide range of booklets. The Prideaux family has served not only as wardens or assistants but for more than a hundred years as clerks. The most famous educational foundation was the Technical and Recreative Institute at New Cross from 1890 to 1904, presented, as Goldsmiths' College, to London University.

Twenty-nine Goldsmiths have been Lord Mayor, Richard Martin serving twice, in 1589 and 1594.

Goldsmiths' Hall, on its magnificent island site in Foster Lane, on the north of Cheapside, is more familiar than most livery company halls through continuous open exhibitions of gold, silver and even porcelain. There have been four halls on the site, dated respectively 1340, 1407, 1634 and 1835. The Roman stone altar to Diana is but one of the many treasures.

Book: *History of the Twelve Great Livery Companies*— Volume 2; W. Herbert; reprinted 1968.

Colours: white and red.

Grocers (2)

The Pepperers, the Grocers' forerunners, were listed in 1180 as one of the adulterine or unlicensed guilds. The Pepperers were congregated around Soper's Lane, now Queen's Street. On 9th May 1345 a fraternity of St Anthony was founded, and the ordinances contained more than the usual rules for the conduct of a craft stipulating, for example, that the wardens should be crowned with chaplets and, rather charmingly, establishing the present-day invitation to ladies by ruling: 'and that every Member having a wife or companion should bring her to Dinner or une damoisele in her place should she be ill, or being great with child and just near her delivery without ony other exemptions'.

The company charters start with Henry VI in 1428 and finish with George I in 1722. The company's control of spices and drugs was established by the official garblers who were nominated by the company, appointed by the Court of Aldermen, to check fraud by the compulsory cleansing of the goods. Obviously the most outstanding Master was in 1689 when on 22nd October King William III accepted the office of Sovereign Master; William Pitt became an honorary freeman in 1784. The company is the governing body of Oundle, the school in Northamptonshire founded by Sir William

Laxton, Lord Mayor and eight times Master of the company, in his will of 1556.

Eighty-three Grocers have served as Mayor or Lord Mayor since 1231, several serving for two, three, four, six or seven years, like Andrew Bokerel (whose residence Bokerel's Bury survives as Bucklersbury), who served from 1231-37.

The company has had five halls on its site in Princes Street, EC2, opposite the Bank of England, dated 1428, 1682 1802, 1890 and 1965. Tragically the fourth hall was destroyed by fire on 22nd September 1965 and the present hall was completed for occupation by November 1970. The Bank of England itself, which started life in 1694 in the company of Mercers' premises transferred to Grocers' Hall in October and operated there until 1734. The new hall is more compact and has an exquisite drawing-room or library containing some superb glass, and a well designed court room with a bust of Pitt looking remarkably like a twentieth-century premier!

Book: *Some Account of The Grocers' Company;* Baron Heath; 1869 (out of print).

Colours: white and red.

Gunmakers (73)

The Gunmakers' is a younger craft, obtaining its charter on 14th March 1637 but not enrolled until 1656. The aims in 1637 remain unchanged today, in that the company is entrusted with the proof of small arms, tested in its Proof House in Goodmans Field, Whitechapel, the only City livery building of its type outside the square mile. The company was granted a supplementary charter in 1892. The legislation of 1855 and 1868 protecting the public from unsound guns upheld the company's charter. The livery includes leading military figures like Field Marshal Sir F. W. Festing and authorities on small arms like W. Keith Neal.

The present address of the Proof House is 48/50 Commercial Road and the oldest part dates from 1757. The hall adjoining was built in 1872 and sold in 1927. Apart from the actual galleries where the guns are tested the building has a court room incorporated in 1952. Among the company treasures is a touch plate of proof marks of gunmakers.

The Gunmakers' mark is unchanged at G.P. crowned.

Colours: not known.

Haberdashers (8)

The Haberdashers were originally part of the Mercers' Company, divided into the haberdashers of hats and of small wares known as millianers or milliners, a word derived from their importing from Milan.

The first ordinances date from 1371 and the first charter 1448 to the Fraternity of St Catherine the Virgin of Haberdashers of the City of London. The charter of 1502 united the two sections. The first grant of arms dates from 16th July 1446 and is one of the earliest known. The main educational charity is William Adams's which founded a free grammar school in Newport, Shropshire, which has had a first-class academic record—and where Dr Samuel Johnson's application as pupil and assistant usher was rejected. The company appoints governors to the four Haberdashers' Aske's schools although, as with many other excellent schools, the operation of the 1944 Education Act brought complications which traditional prestige and excellent administration have had to overcome.

Prince Arthur of Connaught served as Master in 1835. The beadle from 1911 to 1934 was Lieutenant Colonel Croydon, MC, DCM, who was a sergeant major, beadle in 1911, acting brigadier and substantive lieutenant colonel in 1919 and then beadle again.

Forty-one Haberdashers have served as Lord Mayor including Sir William James Richmond Cotton, MP (Master 1874), one of the members of Lord Derby's commission.

The company inherited its present site in Staining Lane off Gresham Street (formerly Maiden Lane) in 1478 and the first hall was destroyed in 1666, rebuilt two years later, damaged by fire and rebuilt in 1840, damaged by fire and again rebuilt in 1864 and completely demolished by enemy action on 29th December 1940. The present hall was completed in June 1956 and contains paintings by Sir Joshua Reynolds, Sir Godfrey Kneller and others, the company records, the figurehead of the company's barge, and some excellent clocks and furniture.

Book: *A Short Description of The Worshipful Company of Haberdashers;* Commander H. Prevett; 1971 (privately printed).

Colours: white and blue.

Horners (54)

One of the oldest of the medieval crafts, the Horners' first known ordinance dates from 1284 followed by others in 1391 and 1455. They were chartered in 1638 and the Grant of Livery was made in 1846. It was formed for the better order of trade and fellowship and its early control was declining at the end of the seventeenth century when a bill had been passed to allow the export of rough horns previously prohibited from 1465. The company revived as a City body from the mid nineteenth century. The Horners' Company is amongst those taking advantage of changing circumstances by appropriately including the plastics industry. Four Horners have served as Lord Mayor.

The company had a hall from 1604 but it was sold in 1879.

Book: *A Short History of The Worshipful Company of Horners;* F. J. Fisher; 1936.

Colours: white and black.

Innholders (32)

Inns became popular with the establishment of pilgrimages; foreign merchants were only allowed in for forty days, during which they had to sell all their stock. Innholders, known as hostelers, were founded in the thirteenth and fourteenth centuries and the company's charters date from 1515, 1664, 1674 and 1685. Formed for trade protection they have little direct connection today and their practical sphere and influence ended with the railways. The company administers an old people's home and grants and scholarships. Three outstanding Masters were William Waterhouse (1820), William James Chaplin (1854-55) and Benjamin Worthyhorne (1858-59), the two latter seeing the end of the coaching era. Three liverymen have served as Lord Mayor.

The freehold of the hall in College Street was acquired in 1613 and the hall was destroyed in 1666, rebuilt four years later and rebuilt again because of disrepair in 1886. It was destroyed in 1941 and rebuilt in 1950. The company's plate includes a collection of Julian spoons from 1539.

Book: *A History of The Innholders' Company;* Oliver Warner; 1962.

Colours: white and blue.

Ironmongers (10)

There were 'feroners' or dealers in iron in London around 1300, more than a century before the incorporation by charter in 1463, confirmed in 1558, 1560, 1604 and 1687.

Originally they traded in and around Ironmonger Lane, Cheapside. The constitution stipulates members may not belong to, or join, other companies, and the court is identical with the livery, the body of yeomanry being retained. Izaak Walton was admitted in 1618, and Thomas Dekker (*c*.1571-*c*.1641), the playwright, wrote the company's pageant for the 1629 Lord Mayor's Show; the Duke of Norfolk is a present member of the court; four generations of the Adams Beck family have served as clerk from 1834 to 1972.

Lord Mayors include William Beckford twice, in 1762 and 1769, and he is commemorated in Guildhall by a statue inscribed with a Remonstrance Speech to the king, not thought, however, to be the speech he delivered! He died in office, with his friend Lord Chatham, according to Walpole, forcing his way into his mansion in Soho Square to retrieve his letters.

The first hall in Fenchurch Street was bought in 1457, rebuilt 1587, rebuilt again 1745-50, damaged by German aircraft 7th July 1917 and later pulled down and the site sold. The attractive Tudor-style hall was built in 1925 in Shaftesbury Place, Aldersgate Street, was restored after war damage, and stands delightfully in the concrete canyons of the Barbican.

Books: *Worshipful Company of Ironmongers;* Edward Hawkes; 1896. *A Brief History;* T. C. Noble; 1889. *Some Account of the Worshipful Company of Ironmongers;* John Nicholl; 1866.

Colours: white and red.

Joiners and Ceilers (41)

There is a reference to William le Joynier in 1239 and the guild of St James Garlickhithe dates from 1375; the company's charters are dated 1571 and 1684, restored 1688. At first the control of the trade was total, but from the seventeenth century onwards appointments to the livery were made of those interested in the City as well as with the trade. The company was associated with the Carpenters' Company in 1893 in the Building Craft Training School, rebuilt 1970. In 1577 Edward Chapman, a master of the Queen's Joynours, served as Master.

Three Joiners have served as Lord Mayor including the libertarian and libertine John Wilkes in 1774 (Master 1770). The company had a hall from the mid sixteenth to the late eighteenth century; in 1578 it purchased a rare Breaches bible, rebound in 1901 and still held.

Book: *The Worshipful Company of Joiners and Ceilers or Carvers, A Chronological History;* Sydney E. Lane; 1969.

Colours: white and red.

Leathersellers (15)

The Leathersellers' Company was formed as a trade guild to regulate the craft and prevent and punish dishonest practices. Its principal charters date from 1444, 1559 (destroyed in a fire), 1604 (the operative charter) and 1685, but as early as the thirteenth century there was a Fraternity of Tanners and White Tawyers, and the company probably succeeds the Gray Tawyers or Tanners and the White Tawyers or Whittawyers, who worked with the Pelterers or Skinners. The 1372 ordinance prevented fraudulent dealings in dyeing or staining of inferior leather. Close trade connection is maintained by establishing and maintaining the Leathersellers' Technical College in Bermondsey, re-established in September 1951 as the National Leathersellers' College. The company are the trustees of the seventeenth-century Colfe Foundation and provide trustees for the famous Colfe's Grammar School for six hundred boys at Lee.

There have been six halls, the first (1447) on company land at Copthall Avenue, London Wall, and the others in St Helen's Place, dated 1543, 1799, 1820, 1878 and 1959. The present livery hall is almost a cube room and approximately half the area of the fifth hall. The assembly hall displays the various ordinances and charters.

Book: *History and Antiquities of the Worshipful Company of Leathersellers;* William Henry Black, FSA; 1887 (out of print).

Colours: white and red.

Loriners (57)

The Loriners were the makers of bits, etc., for horses and may have acquired their name from the province of Lorraine in France. In 1320 there was great bitterness between the Saddlers and the Loriners; in 1448 a bill was presented to Henry IV; in 1511 a petition was presented in Henry VIII's reign to the Mayor and aldermen about bits from France; in 1570 the company was allowed to search for bits of foreign manufacture but not to seize them without the order of the court; in 1597 the Loriners with other guilds were excused their feast because of 'scarsity and dearth'. The early aims of the guild were to prevent the sale of foreign bits and thus to protect the English industry.

Book: *The Loriner . . . Opinions and Observations on Bridle-bits . . .;* Benjamin Latchford; 1871.

Colours: white and blue.

Makers of Playing Cards (75)

The company was incorporated by charter of King Charles I on 22nd October 1628 and its livery was granted by the Court of Aldermen on 27th November 1792. The company was incorporated to protect the manufacturers of playing cards, mainly concentrated in the city of London, against the importing of cards from abroad and against inferior products in Britain. The company had the power of search anywhere in England and Wales, but had to pay the king two shillings on every gross of playing cards made and sealed and a further one shilling per gross to the officer appointed to receive the same and for sealing the cards. Known as the King's Receiver of Composition of Monies he was made a freeman of the company and had an office in the City. In 1897 the company produced a special pack of cards for Queen Victoria's Jubilee, the Queen and the Prince of Wales each accepting a double pack. The Master that year was H. D. Phillips, a member for fifty-two years and serving as Master for the third time. In 1907 he presented his collection of playing cards which is now kept by the company in Guildhall Library. Special issues of cards have been made both annually and for special events; the company had issued a different designed pack of playing cards every year since 1882.

Colours: white and red.

Masons (30)

1972 saw the company celebrate the quincentenary of the grant of the company's arms in 1472 when it was formed to control almost completely and to regulate the stone trade in the City, to further the craft of stone-masonry and to uphold its traditions. Two centuries before the grant of arms two Master Masons and two Master Carpenters had been chosen as City Viewers to inspect walls and gates of the

City. The company charters date from 1677, 1688 and 1702. The company maintains today its old association with the Mercers, Cooks and Broderers. In 1585 it absorbed the Marblers.

History and tradition, in France as in England, caused no surprise that the company's account books make reference to a lodge of 'Acception' of Freemasons in 1620 and 1621 as the earliest authentic evidence of seventeenth-century freemasonry in London; Elias Ashmole, the antiquary, was summoned in 1682. Links with the trade are maintained by grants towards the tools of every apprentice mason in London, support to the Carpenters' Company's Building Crafts Training School, and by the ceremonial reception by the renter-wardens and court of a sailing barge with a consignment of Portland stone for the repair of St Paul's Cathedral. An outstanding Master has been A. F. Philpots in 1972, after serving as clerk from 1947 to 1969, and the company's clerkship has passed from partner to partner in the one firm of solicitors, now known as Hunters, from 1741 to date. One Mason has served as Lord Mayor.

The company had a hall from 1463 to the Great Fire in 1666 and the subsequent hall, in what is still known as Mason's Avenue off Basinghall Street, was sold in 1865.

Books: *The Hale Craft and Fellowship of Masonry;* E. Conder, 1894 (out of print). *The Worshipful Company of Masons,* Raymond Smith (privately printed).

Colours: white and black.

Honourable Company of Master Mariners (78)

The Grant of Livery by the Court of Aldermen was presented in 1931 to the first Master, the Prince of Wales, later the Duke of Windsor, and today the Queen is Patron and the Duke of Edinburgh Admiral. The first court meeting had been held in 1926 and in 1928 King George V bestowed the title of 'Honourable' upon the company. It was the first time in over two hundred years that guildry had admitted a new company. Any master mariner of British nationality of at least five years' competency is eligible for membership and at least twelve of the thirty-six Assistants must be actively afloat. This is another good example of a younger company carrying out strictly the traditions of five hundred years ago.

Outstanding Masters have been Edward, Prince of Wales (1928-36) and the Duke of Edinburgh (1954-57). The company publishes the journal and the pocket book and diary free of charge to members and the semi-annual extracts in booklet form distributed free to British merchant ships.

In 1947 the company had the unique opportunity of acquiring, appropriately, the only livery hall on the Thames, when it purchased from the Admiralty the sloop *Wellington*, berthed permanently since December 1948 at Temple Stairs; its accommodation includes a library and model room.

Colour: royal blue.

Mercers (1)

As one would expect from the company first in order of precedence, the Mercers' company has played a leading part in the history of the City and indeed of England. The charters are dated 1394, 1425 and 1559, the latter being the only one still in existence. The original aims were fully religious, social and trade and although the individual members were all merchants the company exercised only moderate control over their activities. The name Mercer is derived from the French for merchant.

Its three outstanding Masters have been Richard Whittington in 1395, 1401 and 1408, Sir Thomas Gresham in 1569, 1573 and 1579 and Lord Baden-Powell, the founder of the Boy Scout movement, in 1913. Gresham is famous for the Royal Exchange, Gresham College and Gresham's Law and Whittington was later immortalised in perhaps the most famous British pantomime, the first performance of which was given at Covent Garden in 1814. The company administers the Whittington charity, founded by Richard Whittington in 1424, consisting of almshouses, pensions and grants in aid. The company's first-rate record in education is dominated by St Paul's School (founded by John Colet, Dean of St Paul's, in 1508), formerly at the east end of St Paul's Cathedral but transferred in 1884 to Hammersmith; with a new school opened on the river at Barnes in 1968; and the company's own grammar school, Mercers' School, founded in 1542 but closed after the Second World War. The Mercers dominated the Merchant Adventurers Company in the fifteenth and early sixteenth centuries and the only medieval records are at Mercers' Hall. Among the many present distinguished members are Prince Philip, Duke of Edinburgh, Field Marshal Viscount Montgomery and Admiral of the Fleet the Earl Mountbatten.

Sixty-seven Mercers have served as Lord Mayor and the first three Mayors, Henry FitzAlwyn (1192-1211), Roger Fitz-

Allan (1212-1214) and Serlo le Mercer (1215 and 1218-1221), are claimed by the Mercers; twelve others have served for more than one year including Richard Whittington in 1397-8, 1406-7 and 1419-20.

The company originally had accommodation in the hospital of St Thomas of Acon founded by the sister of Thomas Becket to commemorate his birth; the company purchased part of the ground between 1517 and 1524 and built a hall used until 1666, and in 1542 bought the rest of the hospital buildings including the church, henceforth known as the Mercers' Church, from Henry VIII. The second hall was dated 1682 and the third 1958. The hall is unique in now being the only livery hall with its own chapel, in traditional City style, with an ambulatory containing a tomb and an inspiring statue of Christ found during excavations. It was the first home of the Bank of England, and in 1717 was used to start an insurance company known as Mercers' Hall Marine Company and later the Royal Exchange Assurance. Ned Ward reported watching the drawing of lotteries in Mercers' Chapel in 1703!

Colours: yellow and red.

Merchant Taylors (7 and 6)

The Guild of Merchant Taylors of the Fraternity of John the Baptist in the City of London developed from a religious fraternity to a craft association of Taylors and Linen Armourers, receiving their first charter from Edward III in 1327 and the first grant of arms and crest in 1481, confirmed in 1530. The company is the governing body of Merchant Taylors' School, the independent public school founded by the company in 1561; it is additionally interested in three other schools and amongst its charities maintains awards, many scholarships and grants, and three estates of almshouses in Lee and Lewisham, and is the patron of two London churches.

Among the more recent Merchant Taylors to serve as Lord Mayor has been Alderman Sir Peter Studd (1970-71).

The large hall at 30 Threadneedle Street stands on the same site as the first hall of between 1347 and 1392. This was gutted by the Great Fire and September 1940 saw extensive damage from bombs. It reopened in March 1959. The Great Kitchen has been continuously used since 1425 and parts of the three original floors have been preserved in the present floor of the hall.

Books: *Memorials of the Guild of Merchant Taylors; Early History of the Guild of Merchant Taylors;* C. M. Clode; 1875 and 1888.

Colours: white and red.

Musicians (50)

Although musicians have been employed in the City from 1334 as waits, charitable ordinances date from 1350, and established minstrels wore the king's livery in the fourteenth and fifteenth centuries, it was not until 1469 that a rather ineffective charter was granted which applied to the whole kingdom except Chester and which was open to women as well as men. The sixteenth century saw protracted disputes between City Minstrels and the King's Minstrels and the two groups each received charters in the seventeenth century. The King's Minstrels were extinct by 1679 and in 1950 a charter was granted to the successors of the City company. The original aims had been, of course, protection from foreign and itinerant minstrels. The company now gives many scholarships, has a stained glass window in Guildhall, and possesses a collection of manuscripts of early twentieth-century music, including Elgar's 'Dirge', later expanded into 'Elegy for Strings'. Membership today includes many professional musicians including Sir John Dykes-Bower, Professor Herbert Howells and Isadore Godfrey.

Recent Lord Mayors have included Alderman Sir Gilbert Inglefield.

Book: *A Short History of the Worshipful Company of Musicians;* H. A. M. Crewdson; 1971.

Colours: blue and red.

Needlemakers (65)

Cromwell's charter of 1656 made the Needlemakers' the only company not originally incorporated by a monarch. Another charter was granted in 1664 and its municipal rights were granted in 1712. Its control over the trade was complete in its early days. By 1874 the company was revitalised by a group of professional men and MPs interested in the City of London, some of whom gave evidence to Lord Derby's commission.

Book: *The Worshipful Company of Needlemakers of the City of London;* 1876.

Colours: white and blue.

Painter-Stainers (28)

The Fraternity of Stainers, or painters on cloth, dates from 1268 and that of Painters on wood from 1283. The two bodies were joined in 1502 and in 1575 the guild petitioned Queen Elizabeth against the painting of non-apprentices so that the guild was incorporated six years later. Among the disputes in which the guild has engaged was one with the College of Heralds from 1588 to 1738 over the right to paint arms. Over the years members have included such eminent painters as Sir Peter Lely, Sir James Thornhill (Master 1720), succeeding Presidents of the Royal Academy from Sir Joshua Reynolds, the first President, and distinguished public figures like the seventh Duke of Wellington and Sir Anthony Wagner, Garter King of Arms. Between 1947 and 1967 five members of the Court served as Lord Mayor.

Painter-Stainers' Hall, at 9 Little Trinity Lane, was originally left to the guild in 1532 by Alderman Sir John Browne, Serjeant-Painter to Henry VIII. A new hall was built in 1670 after the Great Fire and in 1930 the south wall, three feet thick, which had survived the Great Fire, was condemned for inefficient foundation. Fire damage of 1941 could not be rectified until 1960. The stained glass windows depict the arms of eight liverymen who have served as Lord Mayor.

Book: *The History of the Painter-Stainers' Company of London;* W. A. D. Englefield; 1923.

Colours: white and blue.

Parish Clerks

Although not included in the City livery companies, the Fraternity of St Nicholas, existing from 1274, received a charter from Henry VI in 1442 and later charters date from 1448, 1475, 1610 and 1639. The aims were to establish for ever a Fraternity of Parish Clerks of London, and today membership is restricted to the Parish Clerks of the one hundred and fifty qualifying parishes. The company printed the Bills of Mortality from 1625 to 1858. The company's Visitor is the Bishop of London, its Patron the Archbishop of Canterbury, and the Master with his wardens is Crucifer at the Michaelmas service in St Lawrence Jewry before the election of the new Lord Mayor. The company possesses an obituary roll of the Fraternity of St Nicholas between 1449 and 1521. Four members have served as Lord Mayor since 1919.

The company's hall was destroyed in the Great Fire and the third hall, dated 1671, at 24 Silver Street, was destroyed by enemy action on 29th December 1940.

Book: *The Parish Clerks of London*; R. H. Adams (Clerk of the Company); 1971.

Colours: yellow and blue.

Pattenmakers (70)

Pattens and galoches are mentioned in 1306. Pattens, similar to many fashionable shoes today, were designed to raise the feet above the level of the mud of the streets; they were still worn by the fisherwomen of Ostend a few years ago. The main charter dates from 1670, the supplemental charter from 1960 and the grant of livery from 1717. Originally the type of wood used in pattens was regulated; the patten trade was dead by the end of the eighteenth century and by 1873 the number of freemen had dropped from fifteen hundred to twenty. In 1902 the equipment of the last pattenmaker was purchased by the company. In 1917-18 began the association with the manufacturers of rubber galoches.

In 1961 the court supported the restoration of the church of St Margaret Pattens (now believed to refer to a benefactor Patynz or Patins).

Book: *History of the Worshipful Company of Pattenmakers of the City of London;* Charles; revised Lieutenant Colonel D. A. Davies, 1962.

Colours: white and red.

Paviors (56)

Paving in the City is mentioned in 1280 and four surveyors were appointed in 1311. The company's code and ordinances date from 1479, the charter from 1672 and a grant of livery from 1900. The original aims were to keep out foreigners. The company languished from 1845 but was revitalised in 1889 and many members are now connected with highways and pavings. Since 1922 the company has been a member of the Permanent International Association of Road Congresses. Five Paviors have served as Lord Mayor since 1910.

Book: *History of the Worshipful Company of Paviors;* Charles Welch; 1909 (third edition, 1966).

Colours: white and black.

Pewterers (16)

Pewterers were mentioned in 1348; the company's accounts date from 1451, the first of eleven charters from 1473, and the confirmation of Arms from 1451. Until the end of the seventeenth century pewter was the main material for the table, and the company exercised supervision over the craft, for example, the assay master in a 'coinage' town cutting off a 'coin' or corner of a piece to determine the amount of slag in the alloy. The company's influence declined from the end of the seventeenth century but today it has established a mark to be applied only to the best pewter. Three Pewterers have served as Lord Mayor.

In 1484 the company acquired land, still held, in Lime Street on which the first hall stood from 1495 until 1666. Rebuilt in 1670 it was being let in 1800, damaged by fire in 1840 and demolished in 1932. The company exchanged its site in Queen Victoria Street for the present land in Oat Lane near St Paul's, and opened the new hall on 15th May 1961 incorporating the panelling and chandeliers from Lime Street.

Book: *History of the Worshipful Company of Pewterers;* Charles Welch; 1902.

Colours: yellow and blue.

Plaisterers (46)

The Plaisterers were incorporated in 1501 and were often involved in disputes over the incorporation of painting in their work; for example with Painter-Stainers and, in 1632, with the Carpenters and Joiners. In the nineteenth century the company was considering enlarging its sphere of activities but also found difficulty in arranging an exhibition without the necessary technical knowledge of the craft.

71

William Elder, a Plaisterer, gave a house in Addle Street for a hall, which was destroyed in 1666. It was rebuilt, afterwards let out, and again destroyed. In 1970 a new hall was opened in London Wall, in striking contrast to the Roman wall itself nearby.

Book: *Legends of the Plaisterers Co.* (in verse); 1886.

Colours: silver and turquoise.

Plumbers (31)

The Guild of Plumbers was well established when it received its grant of ordinances in 1365. The ordinances of 1488 enjoined every journeyman to bring with him a hammer, knife and shaving hook on penalty of fourpence. The company's charter was granted in 1611, withdrawn and replaced in 1688, and the original charter restored by William and Mary. It upheld the standards of the trade, including the supervision of weights and scales, the right of search into plumbers' workshops, and the seven-year training of apprentices. The company had the privilege of stamping weights until 1599.

From 1875 the company was revitalised through the agency of George Shaw, Master in 1878 and Chief Commoner in 1879. By 1886 his and the guild's efforts led to the Register for Plumbers opened by the company and only Plumbers who have satisfied the company of their competence are entitled to style themselves Registered Plumbers with the letters RP after their names. During the First World War the services of the company for munitions, particularly with the technique of lead burning, were immense. The company is working to a statutory register of plumbers. Three members of the company have served as Lord Mayor since 1909.

The company had a hall in Chequer Yard, Bush Lane, from 1639 until 1863 when Cannon Street station was built.

Book: *Short History of the Worshipful Company of Plumbers;* 1965 (privately printed).

Colours: yellow and black.

Poulters (34)

The first ordinances were dated 1368, other ordinances being dated 1440, 1513, 1543 and 1550. The date of the company's charter for two centuries had been thought to be

1504 but this point is shrouded in mystery. The grant of arms was made in December 1634; crest and supporters date from March 1635-36. Poulters were in business in the City as early as 5th January 1300 and in 1475 the Poulters appropriately lined the Poultry, where they traded, for Edward IV's procession. Later charters are dated 1665, 1685, 1688 and 1692. The company no longer controls the poultry trade in the City, but significantly, about forty per cent. of the livery are drawn from the trade in Leadenhall and other Markets.

The principal charity is Nepton's, Thomas and Anne Nepton, to whom each year a silent toast is drunk. Three times Masters have died in office, in 1649, 1933 and 1973. One of the outstanding Masters has been the late Colonel Sir Ambrose Keevil, former High Sheriff of Middlesex. The Poulters and the Butchers presented plaques for the centenary of Smithfield Market for the best stall. The present membership includes two of the country's most famous dance band leaders in Geraldo and Edmundo Ros. Three members serve as deputies on the Corporation.

Alderman Sir Joseph Savory, Bt. (Master in 1886, 1887 and 1913) served as Lord Mayor in 1890, Alderman Sir Polydore de Keyser, Kt. (Master in 1891) served as Lord Mayor in 1887, Sir Charles Crossley (Master in 1878) served as sheriff in 1854 and Mr Adam Kennedy Kirk (Master in 1968) served as sheriff in 1961.

The company had a hall between 1616 and 1636.

Book: *The Worshipful Company of Poulters of the City of London;* P. E. Jones (past Master); OUP, 1939 (published privately).

Colour: white and blue.

Saddlers (25)

In 1280 West Chepe, the west end of Cheapside, was known as the Saddlery because there the Saddlers congregated. Until 1548 the collegiate church of St Martin le Grande stood there and amongst the church archives in the custody of the Dean and Chapter of Westminster is a parchment, a convention between the college and the 'Guild of Saddlers' as 'It has been ordained of old between our Church and your congregation' and ending with 'It was also the custom of old'. This establishes the Saddlers as an Anglo-Saxon guild of the greatest age. The company claims to have received its first charter in 1272 from Henry III, and an enrolled charter of a grant of rights from Edward III in 1364; the incorporation charter was granted in 1395 and the operative charter in 1607. These early charters gave the company complete control, including the powers of search, and these searches are still carried out; in the early days the saddles would be publicly burnt at the maker's door. The company presents saddles to overall winners at Badminton and the Royal Windsor and Royal International Horse Shows. The company administers a number of charities and also benefits the craft by the provision of such amenities as stables and sports arenas.

When the Inner London Education Authority deserted Alleyns' School, the Saddlers stepped in to aid this outstanding establishment. Its membership is derived on the basis of three by patrimony to one by redemption, thus retaining the craft guild. It presents the saddle used by the Queen on all ceremonial occasions. It revived in 1962 the category of Yeomen, presented to twelve distinguished users of the saddle; on 30th November 1971 Princess Anne was installed as a yeoman, the year she won the company's saddle at Burghley as individual winner of the European championship. Other distinguished equestrians have also been elected. An honorary assistant is the Duke of Beaufort, Master of the Horse. Perpetual Masters of the company have included Frederick Prince of Wales (1737-51) and the Duke of Connaught (1906-42). Lord Halsbury, Lord High Chancellor of Great Britain, served as Master in 1885 and 1908.

Sir Peter Laurie (1832), Mr William James Richard Cotton (1875) and Sir John Laurie (1941) served as Lord Mayor; William Cotton, formerly alderman of Lime Street and Bridge Without wards, was Master in 1875 and a member of the royal commission under Lord Derby.

The first company hall is referred to in 1479, but it was burnt down in 1666, replaced in 1670, damaged by fire in 1815, and burnt out six years later. The third was destroyed by enemy action on 29th December 1940 and the fourth hall was opened in 1958. It contains some superb plate, paintings, furniture and the magnificent funeral pall dating from the early eighteenth century—6 feet $4\frac{1}{2}$ inches by 1 foot 10 inches of rich crimson brocaded velvet interwoven with gold thread. The company also possesses a most beautiful ballot box dated 1619, made for the East India Company, and so designed that the movement of a cuffed hand dropping a ball into one of the three boxes cannot be discerned.

Book: *The History of The Guild of Saddlers;* J. W. Sherwell

(Clerk); third edition, 1956 (privately printed).

Colours: yellow and blue.

Salters (9)

The bible refers to ' salt of the earth ' and today in certain African countries the highest compliment payable is to say one is loved more than salt. In early days salt was the main food preservative and also imparted taste to dried meats.

The Fraternity of Corpus Christi of Bread Street off Cheapside included many Salters who were living there. The earliest ordinances and a licence from Richard II in 1394 are no longer in existence, nor is the first charter or grant of incorporation dated 1559, but the operative charter, the royal grant of incorporation dated 1607, the confirmation of lands held, dated 1619, and the supplemental charter of 1948 are all held. The early religious and social aims were linked with complete trade control and today the Salters' Company is a stronger fraternity than average, and most of the liverymen are by patrimony.

The Salters' Institute of Industrial Chemistry, founded in 1918, encourages the studies of science at all levels, particularly chemistry; its directors have all been Fellows of the Royal Society, and more than one hundred fellowships have been awarded.

Twenty Salters have been Lord Mayor and Sir Robert Nicholas Fowler, Bt., MP, served twice (1883 and 1885).

The company had halls from 1454 to 1941 when the latest one was destroyed in the Blitz; the site, in St Swithin's Lane, was sold eight years later.

Book: *A History of the Salters' Company*; J. Steven Watson; OUP, 1963.

Colours: white and blue, or blue and red.

Scientific Instrument Makers (84)

This youngest company was formed in 1955, received its grant of arms a year later, and in 1963 the Lord Mayor and aldermen granted their petition as a livery company and the letters patent were handed to the Master the following year. Formed ' to foster scientific instrument making ' and ' to promote goodwill in the craft generally ', the membership is largely restricted to persons originally engaged in the craft or who have obtained a degree of eminence. Instrument-making was formerly under the control of the Blacksmiths until the Clockmakers' charter in 1631. In the second decade of the eighteenth century Robert Bate, a mathematical instrument maker, applied to the Spectacle Makers' Company and the court ruled that he must apply to both companies or stop marketing mathematical instruments peculiarly like clock making!

Outstanding Masters were C. E. T. Cridland, the founder and first Master 1956-57, and G. C. Ottway, Master 1964-65, whose firm has traded in the City without a break since 1640.

Scriveners (44)

There were Writers of the Court and Text Letter in 1357 and the Writers of the Court Letter had their bye-laws seventeen years later; the charter dated 1617 gave them control and administration of their craft, and until the seventeenth and early eighteenth centuries Scriveners were synonymous with notaries. The majority of the Scriveners' Company belonged to the legal or allied professions. Their craft was further protected by an edict of the Court of Common Council in 1752 and legislation in 1801 and 1843; the former act compelled membership on those wishing to practise as notaries in the City, and the latter requires notaries to satisfy the company of their qualification. One outstanding member was Sir Robert Clayton, who had a magnificent palace on the east side of Old Jewry built for his shrievalty in 1671; John Evelyn described it as 'built indeede for a greate Magistrate at excessive cost'. The building was only taken down in 1863. The craft of a Scrivener is not without drama; one scribe late for work with a scratched face reported that a bird cage had fallen on his face! Outstanding Lord Mayors have been Sir Robert Clayton and Sir Robert Shaw.

The company had a hall in Noble Street from 1631 then sold it to the Coachmakers in 1703.

Book: *Scriveners' Company Common Paper 1357-1628;* Francis W. Steer; 1968.

Colours: yellow and blue.

Shipwrights (59)

First mentioned in 1387-88 as a Fraternity of St Simon and St Jude on Thames-side below London Bridge, the ordinances date from 1428 and the charters from 1612 and

1784. For seventy years the company battled with the foreign Shipwrights until their charter, granted 1612, was extinguished in 1684. The livery was given in 1784 and enlarged in 1830. King George VI became Permanent Master in 1932; the Queen has been Patron since 1952 and the Permanent Master is now Prince Philip. The company today maintains strong links with the craft including the holding of three exhibitions.

Sir Frank Alexander, Sir Denys Lowson and Sir Charles Trinder have all served as Lord Mayor.

When the Shipwrights migrated to Ratcliff, Stepney, the company had a hall there from around 1606 to approximately 1794, near the protective towers.

Book: *Records of the Shipwrights' Company;* C. Harold Ridge and A. Charles Wright; 1939 (out of print).

Colours: yellow and blue.

Skinners (7 and 6)

The original Fraternity of Corpus Christi was possibly formed from two groups; the first charter was given in 1327 and others followed in 1392, 1437 and 1667. The guild then controlled the English fur trade until the eighteenth century by the right of search, apprentices, and the high standards of the members. From time to time the wearing of furs has been affected by various sumptuary laws, stipulating the dress to be worn by various ranks of society. There has always been a strong connection with royalty, Richard II and Henry V being two of the five monarchs who have been Skinners. An outstanding Master was Sir Andrew Judd (1533, 1538, 1542, 1547, 1551, 1555), the founder of Tonbridge School, a public school with an excellent tradition, high academic standards and distinction at cricket, as exemplified by Colin Cowdrey, who became a member of the Skinners' Company.

Twenty-five liverymen have served as Mayor or Lord Mayor, two of them twice, and two of them three times.

The original hall, at 8 Dowgate Hill, existed before 1295, vanished in the Great Fire, was rebuilt in 1670 and refaced in 1790; its many treasures include a set of fifteen panels by Sir Frank Brangwyn, RA, depicting the guild's history and achievements, and two illuminated books of the fraternities.

Book: *A Brief Description of the Worshipful Company of Skinners;* Dr Adam Fox; 1968 (privately printed).

Colours: white and red, or yellow and red.

Solicitors (79)

In 1908, when the idea of this company was first mooted, it was almost two hundred years since the last new company, the Fanmakers, had been born in 1709 and almost one hundred years since the Fanmakers had received their livery. On 17th March 1909 a company limited by guarantee and not required to use the word limited was registered under the title The City of London Solicitors' Company. It received its charter as a livery company at the Mansion House on 24th May 1944 and, of course, the limited company was wound up. This is a complete craft guild because it has always been open only to solicitors practising in the City of London and there have been very full discussions as to what is meant by practising. The company has a powerful voice both in collaboration with the Law Society and in the framing of national legislation, and is the local law society for the City. One of its most laudable innovations has been what is called 'The Mad Hatter's Tea Party', where members of the court change places round the table so that each member present has the opportunity to talk to every other member of the court. The company received its grant of arms in 1926. The company has the unique privilege of holding its annual guilds service in the Chapel Royal of St Peter ad Vincula in the Tower of London. The patron saint is St Yves (1253-1303).

Prominent Masters have been Lieutenant Colonel Alderman Sir Cullum Welsh, Sir Thomas Lund and Sir Desmond Heap.

In 1956 Sir Cullum Welsh served as Lord Mayor whilst another member of the court, Sir Charles Norton, was Mayor of Westminster and the next year a liveryman, Mr A. E. Samuel, became chairman of the London County Council.

Book: *The Worshipful Company of Solicitors of The City of London—A Commentary on the Company's Surviving Records;* Arnold F. Steele (past Master, former Clerk); 1968 (published privately).

Spectacle Makers (60)

Spectacle making has not, of course, been confined to Britain and in the mid-fourteenth century Antwerp was an important centre. That the craft had gathered strength in London and learned from confrères in other lands is proved by the grant of the charter in 1629; another charter was granted in 1956. The original object was 'to enforce absolute equality of all the members '. The decline which started at the end of the seventeenth century was arrested two centuries later when the diploma scheme, approved by government committee, was to re-establish the craft as one of the minority exercising today its powers and controls as of yore. The eighteenth century had seen the introduction of telescopes, microscopes, and reflectors and the well-educated apprentices had maintained good relationships with opticians outside the company and at the same time men outside the trade had been admitted; the nineteenth century saw mechanised production. Today the qualification is recognised for any practising ophthalmic optician.

The company had a hall before the Great Fire.

Colours: green and gold.

Stationers and Newspaper Makers (47)

In the 1403 petition the original members are described as writers of text-letters, lymners, bookbinders and booksellers. The first charter is dated 1557 and the latest, 1937, joined the Stationers with the Newspaper Makers. Originally intending to restrict the foreigners, the trade found its course radically changed with the advent of Caxton and printing—more binding and less text writing. During the nineteenth century the Stationers' Company retired from the book trade but is now closely allied to Fleet Street again. The company originally maintained a copyright register, and published almanacks. A school was founded in 1852, opened in 1861 and removed to Hornsey in 1894. Samuel Richardson (1689-1761), the novelist and printer, was elected Master in 1754. Thomas Davis is listed as the only freeman in the seventeenth century to become Lord Mayor, but from 1785 to 1831 nine Stationers served in this office.

The company is said to have had a hall in Milk Street; it had acquired Abergavenny House by 1606, which was destroyed in the Great Fire and rebuilt with other property between 1670 and 1674; damaged in 1940 and restored in 1957, the hall now stands pleasantly in Stationers Hall Court, off Ludgate Hill.

Book: *The Stationers' Company—A History 1403—1959;* Cyprian Blagden; 1960.

Colours: yellow and blue.

Tallow Chandlers (21)

There is a reference to an organisation of Candle Makers in 1300 but the seven charters date from 1462, with the grant of arms in 1456. It set out to regulate the trade, requiring butchers, for example, to sell tallow to chandlers and not to strangers for export. Originally the craft had strong religious associations, as the Church was the biggest purchaser of candles. From the time of George III different lighting methods prevented the previous control. Leading oil and tallow merchants belong to the guild and the London Average Market Letter Committee meets weekly at the hall to note current prices.

Five members have served as Lord Mayor and others as sheriff.

The company had a hall in Broad Street Ward in 1464 and purchased its present site at 4 Dowgate Hill in 1476. It was destroyed in 1666, rebuilt 1672, damaged in the Second World War and completely restored in 1947-55. To celebrate the five hundredth anniversary of the charter the entrance hall was redesigned in 1962.

Book: *A Brief Account of the Worshipful Company of Tallow Chandlers;* Randall H. Monier-Williams; 1968.

Colours: white and blue.

Tinplate Workers (67)

This company is otherwise known as the Wireworkers' and the craft evolved from the Ironmongers' Company. The fourteenth-century records show two separate crafts, joined by 1425, and the company's charter is dated 1670, the grant of livery 1766 and the formal grant of arms 1957. The company originally aimed to stop the importation of foreign tinplate, was active in the seventeenth century, lost control of the trade in the eighteenth century, and was revived in the City form in the late nineteenth century. It has a tradition of visits to appropriate industries for example, in Cornwall and Manchester. Prominent architects of the company were Thomas Aris, Master in 1670, and Dr Ebblewhite who was instrumental in restoring the company's fortunes in the nineteenth century.

Alderman Sir Ralph Perring, Bt., JP, who was Lord Mayor in 1962-63, is a past Master.

Book: *A History of the Tinplate Workers' alias Wireworkers' Company of the City of London;* Oliver Warner; 1964.

Colours: yellow and black.

Tobacco Pipe Makers and Tobacco Blenders (82)

This young guild was granted its charter on 20th December 1960 but it was not the first company. James I had granted a charter of incorporation on 5th October 1619 to the Tobacco Pipe Makers of Westminster which was reincorporated on 10th December 1634 for London, Westminster, England and Wales; this charter was later forfeited and it is thought the company was dissolved in 1642. The second received a charter of incorporation on 29th April 1663, was recognised without a grant of livery on 2nd July, and the company failed two hundred years later for want of members. The present company received its grant of arms on 5th March 1956. On membership the trade participation is extensive. The company grants scholarships to Sevenoaks School.

Book: *History of the Company;* compiled by Alfred H. Dunhill; 1968 (privately printed).

Colours: none stated.

Turners (51)

Warner le Turner is mentioned in the Pipe Roll of 1179-80 and the company's first charter is dated 1604. The guild aimed to regulate its own trade and social behaviour; amongst the goods made by lathe work were measures for ale-houses. The company, like many others, was in decline around 1850, but from the seventeenth century has been supporting the poor, students and charities. It now gives awards for turnery to schools. It has been associated with REME since 1943. Between 1874 and 1949 eight Turners served as Lord Mayor. The company had a hall in 1591 in Philpot Lane, destroyed in 1666, rebuilt four years later and given up in 1737.

Book: *The Worshipful Company of Turners of London;* Roland Champness; 1966.

Colours: yellow and blue.

Tylers and Bricklayers (37)

The company incorporated the existing fraternity and this enabled it to control the trade of tiling—plain, roof and paving—and bricklaying within fifteen miles of the City. Its powers were considerable, including the right of search and imposing fines for bad manufacture and work. Its charters date from 1568 (the first) to 1936 (the fifth). It has its own almshouse charity, now confined to granting pensions. Outstanding Masters were Peter Mills in 1660, a famous architect, a City Bricklayer and, with Sir Christopher Wren, one of the four surveyors to superintend the rebuilding of the City after the Great Fire, and Sir Edward Maufe, RA, the architect, in 1960. 'Rare' Ben Jonson (1573-1637), the dramatist, was a freeman of the company which celebrated the fourth centenary of his birth in 1972.

Two liverymen served as Lord Mayor, Sir Samuel Fludyer, millionaire and enemy of Wilkes in 1761-62, and Sir William Plomer in 1782-83, also his year as Master.

Books: *History of Tylers' and Bricklayers' Company;* Walter G. Bell; 1938 (out of print).

Colours: yellow and blue.

Upholders (49)

Henry le Uphelder is mentioned in 1258 and the company was in existence in 1360. In 1474 a petition was granted by the Mayor and aldermen to give the Upholders right of search and control over feather beds, pillows, mattresses, cushions etc. No one could become a freeman without belonging to the craft which later controlled the trade of general upholstery.

John de Norhampton, Lord Mayor in 1381-82, was an Upholder.

Colours: white and black.

Vintners (11)

First recognised officially as a trade and social guild on 15th July 1364 by a grant of monopoly for trade with Gascony, and with the charters and ordinances given in 1364, 1437, 1611-12, 1619 and 1938 still in existence, the company controlled the trade completely and today's very strong links include awards of a bursary and a scholarship, and the foundation in 1953, with the Wine and Spirit Association, of the Master of Wine examination.

The company's procession each July to St James Garlickhithe after the Master's election is preceded by the white-smocked wine porters sweeping the way. The company gives five cheers instead of three to mark the entertainment, in Henry Picard's year as Master, of five kings—Edward III, of England, David of Scotland, John of France and the kings of Denmark and Cyprus. The swan-upping voyage in July records the numbering and marking of the swans on the

Thames, when the company's swans are marked with two nicks on the beak, and those of the Dyers' Company with one, whilst the Queen's swans remain unmarked. The freemen of the company by patrimony and servitude may sell wine without licence in London and certain other towns.

Of twenty-six Vintner Lord Mayors Reginald at Conduyt held office twice, in 1334 and 1335.

The first hall, dating from before 1446, was burnt down in the Great Fire and replaced in 1667-76 by the present building at 68 Upper Thames Street, EC4, near Southwark Bridge, which has been altered during the years. In Anchor Alley, now Vintners' Place, stands the Coade-stone statue of the Vintry Ward schoolboy, which stood outside the charity school.

Colours: white and black.

Watermen and Lightermen of the River Thames

This company is an active guild but since it is not a livery company it does not figure in the order of precedence. It is regulated by acts of Parliament of 1555, 1603, 1700, 1827 and 1859; Queen Elizabeth granted the arms in 1585. Prior to 1700 the Lightermen had been members of the Woodmongers' Company. The company has always been active and colourful; watermen, like hackney carriages, were for hire. Ned Ward recounted the ad-libbed repartee and invective known as ' river-wit '; from its ranks were drawn the earliest private firemen according to A. E. W. Mason writing in 1920, but he shared the doubts of other authorities of the effect this had on their daily labours and their living; for three hundred years it supplied men for the Navy through impressment; Henry Mayhew in his monumental nineteenth-century surveys interviewed many different types of Watermen and Lightermen in the complex structure and hierarchy, then including the Queen's, the Lord Mayor's, the Admiralty, the Trinity House ' hog-grubbers ', the Navy, and the licensed Watermen with seven-year apprenticeships, entered at Watermen's Hall. It has a strong family tradition amongst its members, who number in thousands, and it is one of the few still carrying out the work for which it was founded.

Some of the eminent freemen include John Taylor (1580-1653) the poet, Ernest Barry, world champion sculler, and Sir Alan Herbert. In 1715 Thomas Doggett, the Drury Lane comedian, gave a Waterman's orange-coloured livery, with a badge representing liberty, to be rowed for by six Watermen within the year of having served their apprenticeship. The race, from the Swan, London Bridge, to the Swan, Chelsea, has taken place every year (in 1777 the course was reversed!); war years are made up after the cessation of hostilities. The Fishmongers' Company provides racing sculls and nominates the contestants to make up the number to six, currently those who have been unsuccessful in previous wagers, and Watermen's apprentices.

The company had a hall in the 1600s, later shown as the Mansion of Cold Harbour on the north bank of the Thames. It was destroyed in the Great Fire, rebuilt in 1670, and again in 1720 on the same site, and the company moved to its present hall at 18 St Mary-at Hill in 1870. The war damage was repaired by 1951 and further improvements made ten years later. Its treasures include a collection of nineteenth century badges. It is the only hall in the Ward of Billingsgate.

Book: *History of the Origin and Progress of the Company of Watermen and Lightermen of the River Thames;* Henry Humphries; 1860 (out of print).

Colours: white and blue.

Wax Chandlers (20)

In 1330 the body called Wax Chandlers collected money for a gift for the king; thirteen years later four men were appointed to check the quality of the wares. The first charter is dated 1483 and the grant of arms was made in 1485 and confirmed with supporters in 1530. In those days the quality of wax was important not only because of the Church but because of such functions as candle auctions. Today the company has close connections with the British Bee Keepers' Association. The Todd family has a hundred and forty years' continuous connections, Dummelow a hundred and seventy, Allt a hundred and eighty, Gregory two hundred, and the Field family over four hundred and sixty.

The site of the company's hall in Gresham Street is mentioned in a deed at the end of the thirteenth century. In 1502 a brewhouse called the Cock on the Hoop was acquired and there are references to a hall in 1545. The Wax Chandlers' Hall is mentioned in 1609, burnt in 1666, rebuilt two years later and in 1791 and again in 1853 because of road widening; it was damaged in 1940 and rebuilt in 1956.

Book: *The Worshipful Company of Wax Chandlers;* Charles D. Todd; 1970.

Colours: white and blue.

Weavers (42)

The Weavers are described as the oldest chartered craft in the City, their charter date starting in 1155 and continuing to 1707. The fraternity is one of those listed as connected with their crafts in the fourteenth century. It had complete control of the weaving industry, for benefit of the Weavers of London, Westminster and Southwark. The fraternity registered in the weavers' ancient book showed that in 1338 householders and journeymen were solidly banded together to withstand the foreign invasions. In the sixteenth and seventeenth centuries there were two major influxes of Huguenot weavers, these being a major factor in changing the main orientation from wool to silk.

The company has provided considerable charitable funds for the advancement, design and technology in the textile industry with scholarships and prizes. An outstanding Master was Samuel Wilson (1832, 1846, 1862 and 1863) who also served as Lord Mayor in 1838 and 1839.

Books: *The London Weavers' Company: from the twelfth century to the close of the sixteenth century;* F. Consitt; 1933. *The London Weavers' Company 1600 to 1970;* Alfred Plummer.

Colours: white and blue.

Wheelwrights (68)

The company was formed to keep out foreigners, that is those not apprenticed, and to regulate the trade. The charter was granted in 1670 and the livery in 1773. By the late eighteenth century the control over the trade had ceased, but from 1882 onwards the company has been a firm supporter of general technical education, by grants and classes. William Shepherd (1894), Lord Edgington of Tatton (1895) and Sir Percy Shepherd (1910) were three of the outstanding Masters.

The company has no hall but it first acquired land in 1948.

Book: *A Short History of the Worshipful Company of Wheelwrights;* 1884 (revised James B. Scott).

Colours: yellow and red.

Woolmen (43)

The Company of London Packers is one of the adulterine guilds of 1180 and the Woolmen are mentioned in 1297 and 1327 in connection with the monopoly of trade. The charter date is 1522. In 1550 there was a fellowship of the Staple; in 1779 the right to license winders and packers was confirmed but this was to be the last practical connection between the guild and the trade. By the eighteenth century the craft was in decline but by 1925 the guild had instituted a scholarship for research on wool at Leeds University. The company still has the right to nominate the recipients of the Merchant Taylors' Vernon Charity. It is reasonable to assume that the woolsack was originally supplied by London packers or the Woolmen's Guild.

Book: *A History of the Woolmen's Company;* H. B. A. Bruyne; 1968.

Colours: white and red.

THE GUILDS

' They were in the nature of benefit societies, from which the workman in return for the contributions which he had made when in health and vigour to the common stock of the Guild might be relieved in sickness or when disabled by the infirmities of age. This character speedily attracted donations for other charitable purposes from benevolent persons, who could not find any better trustees than the ruling members of these communities, and hence arose the numerous charitable gifts and foundations now entrusted to their care. They also possessed the character of modern clubs. They were institutions in which individuals of the same class and families assembled in social intercourse.'

James Anthony Froude (historian, 1818-1894)

' You, my Lord Mayor, occupy a position which is respected, not only in England, but throughout Europe. You represent the municipal principle, to which the civilisation of the world is so much indebted, in its most distinguished form.'

Benjamin Disraeli, Earl of Beaconsfield (1804-1881)

BIBLIOGRAPHY

The City of London; Corporation of London; 1972-73 edition.

City of London Directory and Guilds Guide; The City Press; published annually.

The Corporation of London; Corporation of London; OUP, 1953.

The Craft Gilds of Canterbury; C. F. Bradshaw; City of Canterbury, 1948.

The English Tradition; J. Aubrey Rees; Frederick Muller Ltd., 1934.

The Gilds and Companies of London; George Unwin; Frank Cass & Co. Ltd., 1966.

The Guilds of The City of London; Sir Ernest Pooley; Collins, 1945.

Halls and Treasures of The City Companies; G. W. Whiteman; Ward Locke Ltd., 1970.

The History of The Guild of Saddlers of The City of London; J. W. Sherwell; 1956 (privately printed).

The Livery Companies of The City of London; The City Press, 1962.

The Livery of The City of London; Corporation of London; 1954.

Paintings of the Halls of The City Guilds; Corporation of London; 1963.

Preston Guild Merchant 1972; Frank Billinge; Spinning Wheel Press Ltd., 1972.

The Royal Commission. London City Livery Companies' Vindication; Anon.; Gilbert & Revington Ltd., 1885.

The Soul of The City. London's Livery Companies; Col. R. J. Blackham; 1931.

The Stirling Merchant Gild and Life of John Cowane; David N. Morris; Jamieson & Munroe Ltd., 1919.

The Trades House of Glasgow Handbook; Bell, Aird & Coghill Ltd.; 1967.

The Worshipful Company of Poulters of The City of London; P. E. Jones; OUP.

INDEX

Printed by C. I. Thomas & Sons (Haverfordwest) Ltd., Press Buildings, Merlin's Bridge, Haverfordwest, Pembrokeshire.